Literacy Activity Book

Year 6

Ray Barker and Louis Fidge

EDUCATIONAL

Every effort has been made to trace copyright holders and to obtain their permission for the use of copyright material. The authors and publishers would gladly receive information enabling them to rectify any error or omission in subsequent editions.

Acknowledgements
The authors and publisher are grateful for permission to reproduce the following text:

the extract from *One Hundred and One Dalmatians* by Dodie Smith, published by William Heinemann (a division of Reed Books Ltd); the extract from *Boy: Tales of Childhood* by Roald Dahl, published by Cape, reproduced by permission of David Higham Associates Ltd; the extract from *The Wind in the Willows* by Alan Bennett, based on the story by Kenneth Grahame, by permission of Peters, Fraser & Dunlop; the extract from *I am David* by Anne Holm, published by Methuen Children's Books (a division of Reed International Books Ltd); the extract from *The Secret Diary of Adrian Mole Aged Thirteen And Three Quarters* by Sue Townsend, published by Methuen and reproduced by permission of Random House; the extract from *The Iron Man* by Ted Hughes, published by Faber and Faber Ltd; *Colonel Fazackerley* by Charles Causley published in *Collected Poems* by Macmillan and reproduced by permission of David Higham Associates Ltd; the extract from *The Sword in the Stone* by T.H. White, published by HarperCollins and reproduced by permission of David Higham Associates Ltd; *Facts on Alcohol* first published in the UK by Franklin Watts/Gloucester Press, a division of the Watts Publishing Group, 96 Leonard St, London EC2A 4RH; the extract from *The Eagle of the Ninth* by Rosemary Sutcliff, by permission of David Higham Associates Ltd; the extract from *Global Eye* with the permission of Worldaware and the Department for International Development (DFID); the extract from *The Phantom Tollbooth* by Norton Juster published by HarperCollins Ltd; the extract from *Children at Work* published by the Child Accident Prevention Trust; *Cinderella* by Roald Dahl, published in *Revolting Rhymes* by Jonathan Cape and reproduced by permission of Random House; the extract from *Computerella* by Hazel Edwards, part of the Literacy Links series, published by Kingscourt Publishing Ltd, 20 British Grove, London W4 2NL, reproduced by permission of Mimosa Publications Pty Ltd; the extract from *Getting Things into Perspective* by Colin Caket, published by Thomas Nelson; the extract from *The Machine Gunners* by Robert Westall, published by Macmillan Publishers Ltd; the extract from *The Stones of Muncaster Cathedral* by Robert Westall, published by Viking (1991) © Robert Westall, 1991, reproduced by permission of Penguin Books Ltd; *Macavity the Mystery Cat* by T.S. Eliot published in *Old Possum's Book of Practical Cats* by Faber and Faber Ltd.

First published 1998

Reprinted 1998 (three times), 1999

Letts Educational,
9–15 Aldine Street, London W12 8AW

Tel: 020 8740 2270. Fax: 020 8740 2280

Text © Ray Barker and Louis Fidge

Designed, edited and produced by Gecko Limited, Bicester, Oxon

Illustrations © Sally Artz, James Bartholomew, Michaela Bloomfield, Paul Davies, David Frankland (Artist Partners), Andy Hammond (Illustration Ltd), Robert McPhillips, Chris Molan, Dave Mostyn, Jan Nesbit, Peter Richardson, Martin Sanders, Jamie Sneddon, Ron Tiner, Clara Urquijo (Illustration Ltd). Photograph, page 40, © R.D. Battersby/Bo'sun Photographic Services. **Cover illustrator: Tim Kahane**.

British Library Cataloguing-in-Publication Data

A CIP record for this book is available from the British Library

ISBN 1 84085 066 3

Printed in Spain by Mateu Cromo S.A. Pinto (Madrid)

Letts Educational is the trading name of BPP [Letts Educational] Ltd

Introduction

The Literacy Textbooks:

- support the teaching of the Literacy Hour
- help meet the majority of the objectives of the National Literacy Strategy Framework
- are divided into 3 sections, each sufficient for one term's work
- contain ten units per term, each equivalent to a week's work
- provide two Self Assessment units in each term to check on progress
- contain two Writing Focus units each term to support compositional writing
- include a Glossary of definitions of terms used in the book
- list High Frequency Words at the back of the Year 3, 4 and 5 textbooks
- provide coverage of a wide range of writing, both fiction and non-fiction, as identified in the National Literacy Strategy Framework.

Unit number

Text for reading and discussion

Key teaching points

Text Level activities (purple)

Sentence Level activities (yellow)

Word Level activities (green)

Self Assessment units:

- appear after every five units
- review the key objectives at Sentence Level and Word Level in the preceding five units
- contain a spelling chart to support the teaching of spelling strategies
- may be used to provide:
  - a review of progress when completed and kept as a record
  - further practice in areas of concern
  - homework assignments.

The Glossary:

- explains and gives examples of key words and concepts
- may be used for teaching purposes or for reference by the pupil.

Writing Focus units:

- appear after every five units of work
- develop work covered in the preceding five teaching units
- support work on compositional writing
- contain support for the teaching of different essential writing skills, e.g. how to plan a story.

High Frequency Word lists:

- contain words that occur frequently in children's reading and writing
- help children to recognise these words and to spell them correctly
- are often referred to and used in the activities in the book
- provide an easily accessible resource for spelling activities.

Focus		
Text Level	**Sentence Level**	**Word Level**
• Language affecting the reader	Revision of parts of speech	Unstressed vowels
• Events from a different point of view	Revision of making complex sentences	Roots of words
• Established authors	Dashes and brackets	Prefixes
• Fact, opinion and fiction	Revision of prepositions	Language change over time
• First-person narration	Connecting words and phrases	New words in the language

Writing Focus 1.1   Poetry – figurative language; Narrative viewpoint; Autobiography; Handy hints for redrafting
Self Assessment 1.1   Review of Word and Sentence Level skills Units 1.1 – 1.5; Handy hints for spelling

• Scripts	Revision of verbs and tenses	Suffixes
• Viewpoint of a novel	Active and passive verbs	Origins of names
• Language style	Passive and active verbs	Etymological dictionaries
• Third-person narration	Semi-colons	Spelling strategies – mnemonics
• Selection/presentation of information	Colons	Spelling connectives

Writing Focus 1.2   Writing a playscript; Biography: Being a journalist; Handy hints on making a class newsletter
Self Assessment 1.2   Review of Word and Sentence Level skills Units 1.6 – 1.10; Handy hints for spelling

• Writers evoking response	Active and passive verbs	Word origins and derivations
• Humorous verse	Complex sentences	Spelling rules – dropping the 'e'
• Structure of a text	Revision of clauses	Proverbs
• Argument	Official language – tone and voice	Revision: building spelling by syllables
• Time in a novel	Revision of connecting clauses	Using dictionaries and IT sources

Writing Focus 2.1   Using the text as a model; History and fantasy; Argument; Handy hints for writing an argument
Self Assessment 2.1   Review of Word and Sentence Level skills Units 2.1 – 2.5; Handy hints for spelling

• Suspense	Contracting sentences – summary	Spelling rules – 'i' before 'e'
• Features of a genre text	Conditionals	Mnemonics
• Features of a balanced argument	Note-making	Spelling rules – 'ible' and 'able'
• Using humour for a purpose	Uses of conditionals	Language change over time
• Official language	Official language – words and expressions	Spelling rules – doubling letters

Writing Focus 2.2   'Flashbacks'; Controversial issues; Humour and science fiction; Handy hints for planning a story
Self Assessment 2.2   Review of Word and Sentence Level skills Units 2.6 – 2.10; Handy hints for spelling

• Connections and contrasts	Prepositions and connectives	Roots, prefixes, suffixes
• Comparing texts – value and appeal	Revision of simple to complex sentences	Inventing words
• Comparing texts – styles	Revision of phrases and clauses	Wordplay – jokes and puns
• Features of explanatory texts	Revision of punctuation	Building words – letter strings
• Range of non-fiction text types	How words change meaning	Revision of single or double 'l'

Writing Focus 3.1   Comparison of a theme; Rules and instructions; Reviews; Handy hints for writing a blurb
Self Assessment 3.1   Review of Word and Sentence Level skills Units 3.1 – 3.5; Handy hints for spelling

• Writing style	Revision of active and passive	Revision of short and long vowels
• Comparison of a single writer's work	Derivation	Revision of 'tion', 'sion', 'ial'
• How texts relate to each other	Revision of clauses	Revision of 'er', 'or', 'our'
• Evaluate style of an individual poet	Revision of punctuation	Similes and metaphors
• Retrieving information from a text	Advertising and promotion	Word games

Writing Focus 3.2   Authors; Fiction as a model; Writing appropriately; Handy hints for comparing works by the same author
Self Assessment 3.2   Review of Word and Sentence Level skills Units 3.6 – 3.10; Handy hints for spelling

Term 1

Term 2

Term 3

CONTENTS

Block City

Robert Louis Stevenson lived from 1850 to 1894. In this fanciful poem, he refers to a 'kirk' which is an old word meaning a church.

What are you able to build with your blocks?
Castle and palaces, temples and docks.
Rain may keep raining, and others go roam,
But I can be happy and building at home.

Let the sofa be mountains, the carpet be sea,
There I'll establish a city for me:
A kirk and a mill and a palace beside,
And a harbour as well where my vessels may ride.

Great is the palace with pillar and wall,
A sort of a tower on the top of it all,
And steps coming down in an orderly way
To where my toy vessels lie safe in the bay.

This one is sailing and that one is moored:
Hark to the song of the sailors on board!
And see on the steps of my palace, the kings
Coming and going with presents and things!

Now I have done with it, down let it go!
All in a moment the town is laid low.
Block upon block lying scattered and free,
What is there left of my town by the sea?

Yet as I saw it, I see it again,
The kirk and the palace, the ships and the men,
And as long as I live, and where'er I may be,
I'll always remember my town by the sea.

Robert Louis Stevenson

TEXT

1 Name two things in the first verse that the poet can build with blocks.

2 *a)* How does the poet feel about 'building at home'?

   b) What keeps him feeling this way?

3 *a)* Explain why the steps come 'down in an orderly way'.

   b) Why are the poet's boats 'safe'?

4 Find some evidence that building the city sparks the child's imagination. Give some examples of what he imagines.

5 Do you find what the writer does to the city at the end of the poem surprising? Give your reasons.

6 'This poem is really about the poet looking back on his childhood to talk about his feelings.' Write a paragraph to agree or disagree with this statement.

SENTENCE

1 Write two sentences for each of these words, using the word first as a noun and then as a verb.

   stamp   design   cut   print

2 Write two sentences for each of these words, using the word first as an adverb and then as a preposition.

   behind   up   down   by

3 Make verbs from these nouns, e.g. 'action' as a verb = 'to act'.

   action   spark   bright   song

4 Make nouns from these adjectives, e.g. 'beautiful' as a noun = 'beauty'.

   beautiful   young   high   French

   Write sentences to show these words as both nouns and adjectives.

WORD

1 Write these words, filling in the missing vowels.

   ball _ t   parq _ _ t   cabar _ t   bouq _ _ t

2 Break these words down into syllables, e.g. bus/in/ess.

   company   poisonous   description   freedom   extraordinary   interest   immediate

   Circle the vowels which often get missed out, e.g. comp(a)ny.

3 Looking at how words are derived can help you spell them. Underline the root words, e.g. <u>poison</u>ous.

   description   freedom   extraordinary

   Circle the prefixes or suffixes, e.g. poison(ous).

One Hundred and One Dalmatians

When the Dalmatian puppies are stolen, all the dogs in London and the east of England 'talk' to each other by barking messages. This is called the 'twilight barking'. In this way they are able to find the puppies and tell the puppies' parents.

"Take care of yourself," barked the Sheepdog. "Remember those Baddun brothers are villains."

The cat clawed her way down, backwards, to the ground, then hurried through the overgrown shrubbery. Soon she came to an old brick wall which enclosed a stable-yard. From behind the wall came whimperings and snufflings. She leapt on top of the wall and looked down.

The next second, one of the Baddun brothers saw her and threw a stone at her. She dodged it, jumped from the wall, and ran for her life. In two minutes she was safely back with the Sheepdog.

"They're there!" she said, triumphantly. "The place is *seething* with Dalmatian puppies!"

The Sheepdog was a formidable Twilight Barker. Tonight, with the most important news in Dogdom to send out, he surpassed himself. And so the message travelled, by way of farm dogs and house dogs, great dogs and small dogs. Sometimes a bark would carry half a mile or more, sometimes it would only need to carry a few yards. One sharp-eared Cairn saved the chain from breaking by picking up a bark from nearly a mile away, and then almost bursting herself getting it on to the dog next door. Across miles and miles of country, across miles and miles of suburbs, across a network of London streets the chain held firm; from the depths of Suffolk to the top of Primrose Hill – where Pongo and Missis, still as statues, stood listening, listening.

"Puppies found in lonely house. S.O.S. on old bone –" Missis could not take it all in. But Pongo missed nothing. There were instructions for reaching the village, suggestions for the journey, offers of hospitality on the way. And the dog chain was standing by to take a message back to the pups – the Sheepdog would bark it over the wall in the dead of night.

At first Missis was too excited to think of anything to say, but Pongo barked clearly: "Tell them we're coming! Tell them we start tonight! Tell them to be brave!"

Then Missis found her voice: "Give them all our love! Tell Patch to take care of the Cadpig! Tell Lucky not to be too daring! Tell Roly Poly to keep out of mischief!" She would have sent a message to every one of the fifteen pups if Pongo had not whispered: "That's enough, dear. We mustn't make it too complicated. Let the Great Dane start work now."

So they signed off and there was a sudden silence. And then, though not quite so loudly, they heard the Great Dane again. But this time he was not barking towards them. What they heard was their message, starting on its way to Suffolk.

Dodie Smith

TEXT

1 What did the cat hear behind the wall that told her she had found the puppies? Explain your answer.

2 *a)* What advice did the Sheepdog give the cat?

b) Find evidence to show the advice was right.

3 *a)* Explain the stages by which 'twilight barking' worked.

b) Where did it start and end? How do you know?

4 *a)* Who or what finally received the message? Why were they anxious?

b) What three pieces of information did the message give them?

c) What was the reply?

5 The story is told from the point of view of animals. Find evidence from the passage to support this.

SENTENCE

1 Rewrite these sentences using 'who' or 'which' to join them.

a) The robin returned to her nest. Her nest was in the shed.

b) The rocket flew faster than sound. Sound travels at 335 metres per second.

c) The clown skipped into the ring. The clown made everyone laugh.

2 Use conjunctions, 'and', 'but', 'although' to join these sentences.

a) I like ice-cream. I like chocolate better.

b) It is very hot in the desert during the day. At night it is freezing cold.

c) Helen Keller learned to read and write. She was blind and deaf.

3 Write these sentences but make the sentences more interesting by adding details such as where, why, what, how long to each phrase.

a) We were lost. *b)* I pitched the tent. *c)* This was difficult.

d) I found the necessary tools. *e)* However, we did it.

WORD

1 Use a dictionary to make as many words as you can from these roots.
chair school garden

Underline the root word.

2 Add different endings to these roots to make new words, e.g. 'hard' can make 'hardness', 'hardened', 'hardy'. **child electric construct**

Underline the roots and circle the suffixes.

3 Put your words in sentences to show their meaning.

4 Use the *Look, say, cover, write, check* method to learn these new words.

Macbeth

Do not worry about the words you may not understand. There will be more words you recognise than those you don't. Remember, Shakespeare wrote this 400 years ago. Try to understand the sense of the whole scene.

A Cavern: in the middle, a boiling cauldron.

Thunder. Enter the three witches.

1st witch	Thrice the brinded cat hath mew'd.
2nd witch	Thrice, and once the hedge-pig whin'd.
3rd witch	Harpier cries, "'Tis time, 'tis time."
1st witch	Round about the cauldron go:
	In the poisoned entrails throw;
	Toad, that under cold stone
	Days and nights has thirty one
	Swelter'd venom sleeping got,
	Boil thou first i' th' charmed pot.
All	Double, double, toil and trouble;
	Fire burn, and cauldron bubble.
2nd witch	Fillet of a fenny snake,
	In the cauldron boil and bake;
	Eye of newt, and toe of frog,
	Wool of bat, and tongue of dog;
	Adder's fork, and blind-worm's sting,
	Lizard's leg, and howlet's wing;
	For a charm of powerful trouble,
	Like a hell-broth, boil and bubble.
All	Double, double, toil and trouble,
	Fire burn, and cauldron bubble.
3rd witch	Scale of dragon, tooth of wolf,
	Witches' mummy, maw, and gulf
	Of the ravin'd salt-sea shark;
	Root of hemlock, digg'd I' th' dark;
	Add thereto a tiger's chaudron,
	For the ingredients of our cauldron.
All	Double, double, toil and trouble,
	Fire burn, and cauldron bubble.

William Shakespeare

TEXT

1 Find three pieces of evidence to show this passage is taken from a play.

2 The witches chant their spell. What do you notice about the rhythm and the rhyme of the spell which indicates that it is chanted?

3 *a)* What do all the witches say together three times?

b) What do you think they are doing on stage while they say this?

4 *a)* Write down two disgusting things the 1st Witch adds to the cauldron and four things the 2nd Witch adds.

b) How does this make you feel about the witches? Give your reasons.

c) Why do you think Shakespeare wants you to feel this way?

SENTENCE

1 Write out these sentences, correctly punctuated, using one or two dashes, e.g. He arrived at the bus stop – just in time – to see the bus arrive.

a) The biggest cat last to come in for food licked my hand.

b) My dog lost interest there were no biscuits left.

c) Their holiday six weeks of it was over in a flash.

d) The man was angry all flashing eyes red face and clenched fists.

2 Write out these sentences, using brackets, e.g. He always wore designer jeans (only the best) to school.

a) The cat together with her eight kittens jumped onto the bed.

b) Her Batwoman disguise not a very good one was simple to discover.

c) The teacher awarded him the merit badge first-class work in class.

d) Mum drank her tea ugh! it was cold now and ran for the train.

WORD

1 All these words are to do with numbers.

trio   unique   quartet   millennium   century   decimal   bicycle   octave

Look up their meanings in a dictionary and write them down, e.g. 'century' means one hundred years. Circle the prefixes in the words, e.g. (cen)tury.

2 Find other examples of words using these prefixes, e.g. centenary, centurion.

3 Explain the prefixes for all the words you have, e.g. 'cent' means one hundred.

4 Find and list words using the prefixes 'tele', 'sub', 'micro' from a dictionary. Explain the prefixes.

5 *a)* Use the *Look, say, cover, write, check* method to learn the words in this section.

b) Consider whether adding a prefix changes the spelling of the root words.

Diary of Samuel Pepys

When the Great Fire of London started on 2 September 1666, Samuel Pepys wrote about what he saw and felt in his diary. In this, 'lighters' are small rowing boats and 'virginalls' are musical instruments, like a small piano.

(September 2nd, 1666)... River full of lighters and boats taking in goods, and good goods swimming in the water, and only I observed that hardly one lighter or boat in three that had the goods of a house in, but there was a pair of Virginalls in it..... walked to my boat; and there upon the water again, and to the fire up and down, it still encreasing, and the wind great. So near the fire as we could for smoke; and all over the Thames, with one's face in the wind, you were almost burned with a shower of fire-drops. This is very true; so as houses were burned by these drops and flakes of fire, three or four, nay, five or six houses, one from another. When we could endure no more upon the water, we to a little ale-house on the Bankside, over against the Three Cranes, and there staid till it was dark almost, and saw the fire grow; and, as it grew darker, appeared more and more, and in corners and upon steeples, and between churches and houses, as far as we could see up the hill of the City, in a most horrid malicious bloody flame, not like the fine flame of an ordinary fire ... We staid till, it being darkish, we saw the fire as only one entire arch of fire from this to the other side of the bridge, and in a bow up the hill for an arch above a mile long: it made me weep to see it. The churches, houses, and all on fire and flaming at once; and a horrid noise the flames made, and the cracking of houses at their ruine. So home with a sad heart, and there find every body discoursing and lamenting the fire.

Samuel Pepys

TEXT

1 How can you tell immediately that this is an extract from a diary?

2 *a)* Name two things Pepys saw on the river.
b) Why do you think so many people were trying to rescue their musical instruments?

3 What does Pepys say causes the fire to spread? Describe how this could happen.

4 Some words in the extract keep their old spelling, e.g. 'encreasing' for increasing. Find two more examples of original spelling and write how they are spelled today.

5 The description of the fire is effective because Pepys helps us to feel what he did. List examples from the extract of what he heard, what he saw, and what he felt or touched.

6 A diary is a personal record of events. Make a table to show that Pepys gives us both facts and opinions.

Fact	Opinion
Fire burns	Fire is evil (malicious)

SENTENCE

1 Copy these sentences, underlining the prepositions.

a) The books were piled on the desk. *b)* The racing cars roared around the track.
c) I want to get on the ferry. *d)* The dentist broke into the filling with the drill.

2 Circle the nouns or pronouns to which the prepositions refer.

3 Write sentences using these prepositions.

above   against   after   across   behind   between   over   through   under

4 Use two different prepositions to give each of these sentences a different meaning.

a) The railway line passes _____ the road. *b)* I drove my car _____ the river.
c) Please sign your name _____ the line. *d)* The clown stood _____ the horse.

WORD

1 Look at the extract from Pepys' diary again. Write down any words which we do not use today. What might we use instead?

2 Use a dictionary to find out how these words have changed from their original meanings. Then complete the table.

vulgar   awful   terrific   horrid   villain   nice   pretty

Word	What it means today	What it used to mean
vulgar	lack of taste	ordinary

Boy: Tales of Childhood

Roald Dahl tells us about going away to boarding school when he was nine years old. When he refers to 'tuck', he means food given to children when they left home.

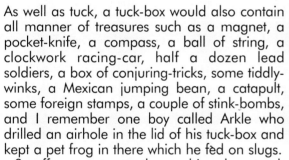

As well as tuck, a tuck-box would also contain all manner of treasures such as a magnet, a pocket-knife, a compass, a ball of string, a clockwork racing-car, half a dozen lead soldiers, a box of conjuring-tricks, some tiddlywinks, a Mexican jumping bean, a catapult, some foreign stamps, a couple of stink-bombs, and I remember one boy called Arkle who drilled an airhole in the lid of his tuck-box and kept a pet frog in there which he fed on slugs.

So off we set, my mother and I and my trunk and my tuck-box, and we boarded the paddle-steamer and went swooshing across the Bristol Channel in a shower of spray. I liked that part of it, but I began to grow apprehensive as I disembarked on to the pier at Weston-super-Mare and watched my trunk and tuck-box being loaded into an English taxi which would drive us to St Peter's. I had absolutely no idea what was in store for me. I had never spent a single night away from our large family before.

St Peter's was on a hill above the town. It was a long three-storeyed stone building that looked rather like a private lunatic asylum, and in front of it lay the playing-fields with their three football pitches. One-third of the building was reserved for the Headmaster and his family. The rest of it housed the boys, about one hundred and fifty of them altogether, if I remember correctly.

As we got out of the taxi, I saw the whole driveway abustle with small boys and their parents and their trunks and their tuck-boxes, and a man I took to be the Headmaster was swimming around among them shaking everybody by the hand.

I have already told you that *all* Headmasters are giants, and this one was no exception. He advanced upon my mother and shook her by the hand, then he shook me by the hand and as he did so he gave me the kind of flashing grin a shark might give to a small fish just before he gobbles it up. One of his front teeth, I noticed, was edged all the way round with gold, and his hair was slicked down with so much hair-cream that it glistened like butter.

"Right," he said to me. "Off you go and report to the Matron." And to my mother he said briskly, "Goodbye, Mrs Dahl. I shouldn't linger if I were you. We'll look after him."

My mother got the message. She kissed me on the cheek and said goodbye and climbed right back into the taxi.

The Headmaster moved away to another group and I was left standing there beside my brand new trunk and my brand new tuck-box. I began to cry.

Roald Dahl

TEXT

1 *a)* List five things you might find in a tuck-box.

b) Explain why these might be 'treasures' to a small boy.

2 *a)* What words show you how the boy felt when he started his journey?

b) How had his feelings changed by the time he had crossed the Bristol Channel?

c) Give two reasons to explain why he felt this way.

3 Write a paragraph to describe Roald Dahl's new school and his new headteacher. How do you feel about them?

4 This extract is from Roald Dahl's own version of his life story (autobiography).

a) Who is telling you the story? Which words does he use that show this?

b) Remembering all that happened to you as a child can be difficult.

What phrase in the passage shows that he is not sure about some facts?

c) Why should he remember so vividly his reaction in the final line?

SENTENCE

1 Reread the passage. *a)* Write down three conjunctions (simple connecting words).

b) Explain which ideas they are connecting.

2 Join the two sentences using conjunctions 'when', 'before', 'although', 'so that'.

a) Fred paused. He spoke. *b)* The leaves were falling from the trees. It was lighter in the wood. *c)* They began to cry. A large dog growled at them. *d)* The box would not squash down. It was only paper.

3 Some connecting words give you an idea of position. Write sentences using 'beside', 'nearby', 'by'.

4 Other connecting words give you an idea of a sequence. Write a list of instructions, e.g. about how to make toast, using 'first', 'secondly', etc.

WORD

1 Use a dictionary to find out how these words came into our language.

sandwich   wellington   guillotine   nicotine   volt   watt   loganberry   saxophone

2 Put them into sentences.

3 Using a dictionary, or other reference sources, what can you find out about the origins of these new words?   **alphabet   bus   pram   fridge   nylon   motel**

4 Many new words have come from America, e.g. ranch, jazz. What would Americans call the following?

● **a flat to live in**   ● **a refrigerator**   ● **petrol**   ● **a lift**   ● **the Underground**

● **the pavement**   ● **a film at the cinema**

Writing poetry

1 Read this poem about a greyhound, which is made up of comparisons, or similes:

> *A head like a snake, a neck like a drake,*
> *A back like a beam, a belly like a bream,*
> *A foot like a cat, a tail like a rat.*

Look at the pattern it makes and how it rhymes. Write a comparison, or simile, poem using this as a model, e.g.

A head like a ... , a neck like a ....

2 Now read this more amusing, simile poem. Write your own, using the example as a model. Look at the pattern it makes and how it rhymes:

> *Imagine a flea, as big as a bee,*
> *Imagine a rat, as fat as a cat,*
> *Imagine a goat, as wet as a boat.*

3 You can use metaphors in poems by using simple patterns. Continue with one of these ideas.

> *Summer is ... an oven*
> *School is ... a prison*
> *Homework is ...*
> *My friend is ...*
> *Red is ...*

Changing the narrative – of view

4 Now imagine that the Sheepdog in *One Hundred and One Dalmatians* (page 8) was writing his diary about the events of the day. Write his diary entry using the information from the passage.

5 Imagine that Samuel Pepys was being interviewed by a television news reporter. Write the interviewer's questions, and how they might be answered. Use lots of detail from the passage.

Autobiography

6 Imagine you are going to publish your autobiography, or life story. Write the first chapter.

Do you really need to say where and when you were born or where you live? Do these facts help people to get a picture of you as a person? Think about some of these:

◆ My schools
◆ Places important to me
◆ My hobbies and interests
◆ My festivals
◆ People special to me
◆ My brothers and sisters

Remember:

Autobiographies do not work through a person's life, event by event. They choose the most important or interesting moments. Tell your reader about events you remember, e.g. your first day at school. You may not think that they are interesting, but your reader will. Then find some photographs to illustrate your work.

Remind yourself of some of the features of an autobiography by reading *Boy: Tales of Childhood* (page 14) again.

Handy hints for redrafting

Audience
Who is the intended audience for your writing? Is the language you are writing in suitable?

Purpose
What is the purpose of the piece of writing?

Form of writing
Story? Diary? Playscript? Autobiography? Newspaper report?

Grammar and punctuation
Have you checked that your sentences are correct? Have you checked for capital letters and full stops? Have you checked the punctuation of speech?

Now redraft and improve your autobiography.

How are you getting on with the skills in the chart? If you need extra practice, try the numbered activities.

Grammar and punctuation	Parts of speech	1
	Making complex sentences	2
	Prepositions	3
	Connecting words and phrases	4
	Dashes and brackets	5
Spelling, phonics and vocabulary	Words containing unstressed vowels	6
	Roots of words	7
	Language change over time	8
	New words in the language	9
	Prefixes	10

1 *a)* Form nouns from these adjectives, e.g. strong – strength:

strong _____ , loyal _____ , good _____ ,
long _____ , wide _____ , ugly _____ .

b) Make adjectives from these nouns by adding 'y' or 'ly':

bush _____ , sleep _____ , beggar _____ ,
king _____ , coward _____ , wind _____ .

c) Write sentences using all these words.

2 Make these simple sentences more interesting by adding the phrases in the box on the right:

Ranjit _____ set out for his holiday. He arrived on Saturday _____ . Shusha _____ welcomed him. Her house _____ looked different. They went into the nearest city _____ . Ranjit _____ bought many souvenirs.

excited to be in the centre of India

trembling with excitement

his mother's favourite sister

a noisy, brightly coloured place

amazed at the wonderful carvings

covered with tropical flowers

3 *a)* By using different prepositions, write out these sentences twice and give each a different meaning:

The railway passes _____ the road. I drove the car _____ the village. The hounds chased the fox _____ the field. The plane was returning _____ Washington. My cat sleeps _____ the chair. The clown jumped _____ the horse. The snow was moving _____ the west.

4 *a)* Write sentences using these simple connecting words:

when   before   as   although   until   so that   because

b) Make a list of all the connecting words you can find. Put them into columns in a chart:

location	order	time	argument	explanation
under	first	then	therefore	because

5 *a)* Rewrite these sentences using dashes and brackets:

He rushed into the classroom the class had gone.

The lottery result it was no business of hers interested her a great deal.

The Easter eggs a dozen of them only lasted a day.

She bought the skirt the last in the sale.

b) Explain why you used brackets or dashes above.

6 *a)* Write out the words: poisonous, freedom, description. Circle the suffix. Say which letter is often missed out when the word is spelled.

b) Write out the words: extraordinary, immediate. Underline the root of the word and circle the prefix. Show how, when you add a prefix, the root of the word does not change.

7 *a)* Write out these words, underlining the root word in each case: playmate, playground, playschool, playtime.

b) Write them in sentences to show their meanings.

c) Make a list of words from these roots: school, foot, head.

8 Words can change their meanings over time.

a) How are these words used today? *b)* What did they originally mean? Look at the clues in brackets:

pop (music), boot (car), park (car), jet (plane).

9 Use a dictionary to find out when these new words came into our language and what they mean: stereo, apartheid, helicopter, hovercraft, trainer, motorway.

10 These groups of prefixes mean opposite things:

pre, post; mini, maxi; anti, pro; sub, sur.

a) Find words that begin with each of these prefixes.

b) Write them in sentences to show their meaning.

c) Explain what the prefixes mean.

Handy hints for spelling

◆ Is the word spelt as it sounds? Does it contain any phonemes you already know?

◆ Does the word look right? Do you know any other words like it?

◆ Can you break the word into smaller parts? Which is the most difficult part of the word?

◆ Do you know what the word means?

◆ Have you used a word book or dictionary to help you?

LOOK
SAY
COVER
WRITE
CHECK

The Wind in the Willows

Mr Toad is being helped by his friends Badger, Rat and Mole to recover from his latest 'craze' – his new love of the motor car.

Toad is at the wheel of his latest motor car, leading an admiring throng of Rabbits and Hedgehogs in a lap of honour around Toad Hall.

Toad **(singing)**	**The Army all saluted As they marched along the road. Was it the King? Or General French?**
Rabbits	**No. It was Mr Toad.**
Toad	**The Queen and her ladies-in-waiting Sat in the window and sewed She cried, "Who's that handsome man?"**
Rabbits	**They answered, "Mr Toad".**

Badger, Rat and Mole march sternly on.

Toad	**Hello, you fellows. Just the people I want to see. How do you like her? Isn't she a beauty? And she goes like a bird. I can't wait to get her on the road. Pile in and I'll show you. What's the matter? Why these long faces?**
Badger	**Rat. Mole.**

Rat and Mole seize him and bundle him away – though Mole (and it is to his credit) finds this more difficult than does Rat.

Toad	**Get off, you fellows. What are you doing? Help! Leggo! You can't frogmarch me, I'm a Toad!**
Badger	**Are you the car salesman?**
Salesman	**I am. Parkinson's the name. Mr Toad is one of our most valued customers.**
Badger	**I bet he is. Well, Mr Toad has changed his mind. He will not require the car. The craze is over.**
Salesman	**Motor cars is not a craze, sir. They are the coming thing. Motor cars is progress, sir. Motor cars is the future.**
Badger	**Not for toads. Good morning, Mr Parkinson.**

Mr Parkinson, who is not used to having his customers kidnapped, goes off in a huff and the new motor car with Toad, who has given his captors the slip, running frantically in pursuit.

Toad	**Stop, stop, where is he going? Where is he taking my beautiful motor?**
Badger	**Back.**
Toad	**Back? How dare you?**
Badger	**Toad. Listen to me. You are suffering from an illness.**
Toad	**Rubbish. I never felt better in my life. Oh, my beautiful motor!**
Badger	**A mania. A sickness of the mind.**
Toad	**Poop poop.**
Rat	**Don't be rude, Toad.**
Toad	**Rude? May I remind you you're on my property.**
Badger	**If you are to recover from this illness it will depend on your being kept away from the source of the infection. Motor cars.**
Toad	**Motor cars are not an infection. Motor cars are my life.**
Rat	**But these crashes, Toad. The fines. The Wild Wooders think you've got money to burn.**
Toad	**So? One can't help being rich. The Wild Wooders don't scare me.**

By Alan Bennett based on the story by Kenneth Grahame

TEXT

1 *a)* What impression do the songs give of Mr Toad? Give your reasons.
   b) What does it show about Mr Toad that he is singing these songs about himself?

2 What reasons do Toad's friends give for taking Toad away from his car?

3 How do Toad and the car salesman react to the reasons?

4 *a)* Explain what you find funny about the extract.
   b) Why is 'You can't frogmarch me, I'm a Toad!' funny?

5 'Badger, Rat and Mole march sternly on.' *a)* What instructions does this stage direction give the characters? *b)* How does it show them how to feel, e.g. why march rather than walk? What is the importance of 'sternly'?

6 Write down three ways a playscript is different from speech written in a story.

SENTENCE

1 Copy this passage. Change all the verbs from the present to the past tense.

We sit at a table in the square. The sun is hot. The sky is clear and blue. Tourists are walking around looking busy. Suddenly we see a tall, dark man. He rushes out of a building to our right. He jumps into a red car. It is obviously waiting for him. The car races into the distance.

2 Copy this passage, changing all the verbs from the past to the future tense.

We arrived in the resort at 10 o'clock and went straight to the sea. It was boiling hot and rain was not expected for a week. We went to a show in the evening and ate at a very grand restaurant. It was a great holiday.

WORD

1 Write these words, dividing them into syllables.
   marching   admiring   waiting   doing   coming   going   morning

2 *a)* What suffix do they all have in common? *b)* Write down the root in each word.
   c) Underline where any spelling changes have happened when the suffix was added.

3 Write these words from the passage, dividing them into syllables.
   saluted   sewed   cried   answered   valued   changed

4 *a)* What suffix do they all have in common? *b)* Write down the root in each word.
   c) Underline where any spelling changes have happened when the suffix was added.

5 What happens when you add 'ing' or 'ed' to words ending in a vowel, e.g. shape? Invent a rule and find five more examples to prove your rule.

I am David

It is the Second World War. David is 12 years old. He has spent years of his life in a prison camp, but has been given the chance to escape.

David remembered all the pain and bitterness he had ever known – and how much he could remember in such a short time! He recalled, too, all the good things he had learned about since he had gained his freedom – beauty and laughter, music and kind people, Maria, and a tree smothered in pink blossom, a dog to walk by his side, and a place to aim for …

This would be the end. He pressed his face into the dog's long coat so that no one should hear him, and wept. He wept quite quietly, but the dog grew uneasy and wanted to whimper again.

David stopped crying. "God," he whispered, "God of the green pastures and still waters, I've one promise of help left, but it's too late now. You can't do anything about this. I don't mean to be rude, because I know you're very strong and you could make those men down there want to walk away for a bit. But they won't. They don't know, you see, and they're not afraid of you. But they are afraid of the commandant because he'll have them shot if they leave their posts. So you can see there's nothing you can do now. But please don't think I'm blaming you. It was my own fault for not seeing the danger in time. I shall run … Perhaps you'll see they aim straight so it doesn't hurt before I die. I'm so frightened of things that hurt. No, I forgot. I've only one promise of help left, and it's more important you should help the dog get away and find some good people to live with. Perhaps *they'll* shoot straight anyway, but if they don't it can't be helped: you must save the dog because it once tried to protect me. Thank you for having been my God: I'm glad I chose you. And now I must run, for if I leave it any longer I shan't have the courage to die. I am David. Amen."

The dog kept nudging him. It wanted them to go back the way they had come, away from the spot where it sensed danger lurking.

"No," David whispered, "we can't go back – it's too late. You must keep still, King; and when they've hit me, perhaps you can get away by yourself."

The dog licked his cheek eagerly, impatiently nudging him again and moving restlessly as if it wanted to get up. It nudged him once more – and then jumped up before David could stop it. In one swift second David understood what the dog wanted. It did not run back the way they had come. It was a sheepdog and it had sensed danger … It was going to take David's place! Barking loudly it sprang towards the men in the dark.

Anne Holm

TEXT

1 *a)* What happy things does David remember while he is trapped?

b) Why should these be different from his life in the prison camp?

2 David realises 'This would be the end' and he cries. What else did he do that meant a lot to him?

3 *a)* What does David want God to give him and the dog?

b) What do you think about the way David spoke to God?

c) What does this prayer show about David's character?

4 What do you think it means that the dog 'was going to take David's place'? What do you think happens next?

5 Write a paragraph explaining how you feel about David's situation, what sort of person you think David is, how well you think he acted and how you think the story will end.

SENTENCE

1 Copy these sentences, changing them from the active to the passive tense, e.g. 'Police guard the Queen' (active) and 'The Queen is guarded by police' (passive).

a) Bad weather delayed our flight.

b) Wearing ear plugs at the disco deadened the noise.

c) The garage carries out services on cars.

d) Shouts directed the police to the girl.

e) He put out his hand for the money.

f) The dog chased the cat around the yard.

g) My sister organised the disco for her wedding.

2 Explain the differences between the two types of sentence. Who/what is carrying out the action in each sentence?

3 In what kinds of writing do you use the active tense more than the passive?

WORD

1 *a)* Look in a dictionary to find the meaning of the word 'surname'.

b) What does the prefix 'sur' mean?

2 Some names originate from the jobs people had. What do you think these ancestors used to do?

Goldsmith   Mason   Archer   Waller   Thatcher   Tyler   Painter   Baker

Give reasons for your answers.

3 The Irish prefixes 'O'' and 'Mac' and the Scottish prefix 'Fitz' all used to mean 'son of', e.g. O'Neill (son of Neill). List three surnames which use each of these prefixes.

4 People used to be given names to describe where they lived.

a) Explain which is the odd name and why.

Wood   Brooke   Baker   Field   Hill

b) Think of three more surnames which represent landscape.

The Secret Diary of Adrian Mole Aged Thirteen and Three Quarters

Adrian Mole is thirteen and three quarters – an age when the extra three quarters can make all the difference. He records his life in diary form.

Tuesday January 27th

Art was dead good today. I painted a lonely boy standing on a bridge. The boy had just lost his first love to his ex-best friend. The ex-best friend was struggling in the torrential river. The boy was watching his ex-best friend drown. The ex-best friend looked a bit like Nigel. The boy looked a bit like me. Ms Fossington-Gore said my picture 'had depth', so did the river. Ha! Ha! Ha!

Wednesday January 28th

LAST QUARTER

I woke up with a bit of a cold this morning. I asked my mother for a note to excuse me from Games. She said she refused to namby-pamby me a day longer! How would she like to run about on a muddy field in the freezing drizzle, dressed only in PE shorts and a singlet? When I was in the school sports day three-legged race last year she came to watch me, *and* she had her fur coat on *and* she put a blanket round her legs, *and* it was only June!

Anyway my mother is sorry now, we had rugger and my PE stuff was so full of mud that it has clogged up the drain hose on the washing machine.

The vet rang up to demand that we come and fetch the dog back from his surgery. It has been there nine days. My father says it will have to stay there until he gets paid tomorrow. The vet only takes cash and my father hasn't got any.

Pandora! Why?

Thursday January 29th

The stupid dog is back. I am not taking it for a walk until its hair grows back on its shaved paws. My father looked pale when he came back from the vet's, he kept saying 'It's money down the drain', and he said that from now on the dog can only be fed on leftovers from his plate.

This means the dog will soon starve.

Sue Townsend

TEXT

1 Describe the picture that Adrian painted.

2 *a)* Explain the joke from the January 27th entry.

   b) Explain two other things that you find amusing in the diary.

3 *a)* How did Adrian's mum embarrass him?

   b) How does Adrian think he took revenge on his mum over his PE kit?

4 *a)* Who is the main subject of the diary? What repeated word tells you this?

   b) What does Adrian write about mainly?

5 Find three examples of verbs. What tense is used? Is this the best tense for a diary? Explain why.

6 Find evidence for these diary features – entries are written at different times, uses 'I' (or the first person), uses the past tense, sounds like a conversation and uses personal details.

SENTENCE

1 Copy these sentences, changing them from the passive to the active tense.

   a) The battery was connected to the mains.

   b) A small amount of sugar was taken and placed in water.

   c) The suitcase is examined by a customs officer.

   d) Children under seven are looked after by nurses.

   e) The money was put into his hand.

   f) The bottle was dropped by the teacher.

   g) Our lawn was cut by the gardener last week.

2 Explain the differences between the two types of sentence. Who/what is carrying out the action in each sentence?

3 In what kinds of writing do you use the passive tense more than the active?

WORD

1 Use an etymological dictionary to find the derivation of the word 'etymology'. Explain how the parts of the word make up its meaning.

2 Find out from which country these words come.

   caravan   yoghurt   sofa   dessert   shampoo

3 In which countries did these sports begin?   **polo   skiing   judo**

4 *a)* Find out the meaning of these words.

   braille   volt   cardigan   spoonerism

   b) Explain the origin of the words. *c)* Put the words into sentences.

5 Write down what you can find from dictionaries about how these words came into the English language.

   dachshund   bayonet   Pekinese   chocolate

Anne Frank Beyond the Diary

This extract is taken from the biography of Anne Frank, whose diary tells of her family's experiences when hiding from the Nazis in Amsterdam during the Second World War.

What did Anne do during those long daytime hours? She spent a lot of time studying her schoolbooks, a large pile of which had been taken along. She also read many books which Miep brought her, and learned shorthand. Margot and Peter also spent many hours on their schoolwork every day. Otto Frank helped all three children and tested them on their lessons. None of them wanted to fall behind in their studies. They still hoped that they would be able to return to school soon.

Many Jews in the Netherlands were picked up during these months and taken to concentration camps. Though the Frank and Van Pels families had escaped this, they could not escape being crowded on top of each other day and night. They saw and heard everything everyone did. This lack of privacy, as well as the never-ending fear of discovery, put everyone constantly on edge. It is therefore not surprising that arguments were a regular part of life in the Annex.

Anne wrote: *Why do grownups quarrel so easily, so much, and over the most idiotic things? Up till now I thought that only children squabbled.* (September 28, 1942)

Anne, too, found her new life difficult. She had lost everything: her friends, her school, her freedom. Sometimes she rebelled, and sometimes sadness overtook her and she often cried at night. But during the day she was different: lively and boisterous, and usually surprisingly cheerful. She had something to say about everything and everyone, and was always ready with a quick answer. Mr and Mrs Van Pels thought her behaviour insolent and believed she had been brought up badly. Edith Frank regularly argued with Anne, and Margot was often short-tempered with her. Peter wasn't much help, either.

Margot and Peter aren't a bit what you would call 'young', they are both so staid and quiet. I show up terribly against them and am always hearing "You don't find Margot and Peter doing that – why don't you just once follow your dear sister's example?" I simply loathe it. (February 5, 1943)

Anne felt truly alone and misunderstood. Her diary had become her one really good friend.

Most of the time life in the Annex was simply boring. Yet there were also moments of great excitement – and great fear. One evening at eight o'clock the bell suddenly rang loudly. Everyone was terrified. Was it the German police, the Gestapo? Was it the end? They all held their breaths. But there was no more noise.

Ruud van der Rol and Rian Verhoeven

TEXT

1 Explain what three things Anne did to stop being bored when hidden away.

2 *a)* How did Anne's father help them? *b)* Explain why they wanted this help.

3 *a)* What does the writer say were some of the results of the overcrowding in the Annex?
b) Why was the diary so important to Anne?

4 *a)* What was Anne like when she was sad? *b)* How was she different during the daytime? *c)* What did Mr and Mrs Van Pels think of her behaviour?

5 Describe one event which frightened the people in the Annex and say what eventually happened.

6 Look at the two sorts of writing in the passage – the biography and the diary entries. Write down three differences between them.

SENTENCE

1 Write out these sentences, putting in semi-colons and any other necessary punctuation, e.g. 'It was March; the snow had fallen suddenly overnight.'

a) As time passed I became more patient soon the train would come.
b) The river was beautiful and calm boats floated over the surface
c) Don't forget to bring the following ingredients an egg which is not too large or brown a bag of brown flour not white or plain and a tin to put the cake in
d) In the cage the lions were asleep in the straw the tiger was pacing up and down
e) We are having these at my party: apple pie and custard cakes bursting with cream fillings chocolate shapes packed with fruit bread and cheese from France
f) They talked a great deal they had not seen each other for a long time

2 Rewrite the sentences using punctuation other than a semi-colon. What could you use? Do you have to change the punctuation or add new words, such as conjunctions?

WORD

1 Explain how the mnemonic 'Never Eat Shredded Wheat' helps you to remember the points of the compass.

2 Which three words do these mnemonics help you spell? 'Mother ants never yell', 'Dads often eat sugar', 'Wasps always sting'. Explain why.

3 Invent mnemonics to help you spell these words:
because   immediately   necessary

4 Write sentences to help you to remember how to spell these words. Look at the clues in brackets.
friend (end)   island (land)   separate (rat)   piece (pie)   hear (ear)

Penny for the Guy

Henry Mayhew was a journalist in the 1850s. He was one of the first people to write about the poor in London. Here he interviews some boys about what they did on 5 November.

I couldn't have been more than seven years old when I first began. They put paper-hangings round my legs – sometimes they bought, and sometimes they got it given to them; but they gave a rare lot for a penny or twopence. After that they put on me an apron made of the same sort of paper – showy, you know, then they put a lot of tinsel bows, and at the corners they cut a sort of tail … it looked stunnin'; then they put on my chest a tinsel heart and rosettes; they were green and red because it shows off. All up my arms I had bows and things to make a showoff. Then I put on a black mask with a little red on the cheek, to make me look like a devil: it had horns, too. Why, he made me a little guy about a foot high, to carry in my lap. It was made to sit in a chair; and there was a piece of string tied to each of the legs and the arms; and a string came behind; and I used to pull it, and the legs and arms jumped up.

I was put in a chair, and two old broom-handles were put through the rails, and then a boy got in front, and another behind; and carried me off round Holborn way in the streets and squares. Every now and then they put me down before a window; then one of 'em used to say the speech, and I used all the time to keep pulling the string of my little guy, and it amused the children at the windows. Then some of them went and knocked at the door and asked "Please to remember the Guy"; and the little children brought us ha'pence and pence; sometimes the ladies and gentlemen chucked money out of the window. At last they carried me into Russell Square. They put me down before a gentleman's house and began saying the speech: while they were saying it, up comes a lot of boys with sticks in their hands.

After a bit one of these boys says "Oh, it's a dead guy; let's have a lark with it!" and then one of 'em gives me a punch in the eye with his fist and then snatched the mask off my face, and when he pulled it off he says, "Oh, Bill, it's a live 'un!" We were afraid that we should get the worst of it, so we ran way round the Square. After we'd run a little way they caught us up again and says, "Now then, give us all your money." With that, some ladies and gentlemen that saw it all came up and says, "If you don't go, we'll lock you up"; and so they let us go away. And so we went to another place where they sold masks and we bought another.

Henry Mayhew

TEXT

1 Describe how the boy was dressed to make him a 'guy'.

2 *a)* What did he have to carry?   *b)* What was special about it?

3 List, in stages, what they did to collect money.

4 *a)* Describe how they were nearly robbed.   *b)* How were they saved?
   c) What did they have to do to carry on?

5 Mayhew interviewed the boys and printed their story in his paper. Should we believe what they have to say or be suspicious? Give your reasons.

6 What differences are there in the ways November the 5th has been celebrated? Find evidence from the passage to complete the table.

1850s	Today
Dress people to be 'guys'	Make a model 'guy'

SENTENCE

1 Rewrite these sentences, correctly punctuated, using a colon where necessary, e.g. 'Remember to bring these for the exam: a pencil, pen and a ruler.'

   a) He had not done enough work for the test he would fail
   b) Unfortunately he did not have a choice he would have to sell his car
   c) Please note no dogs allowed   *d)* My mum screamed its a mouse its a mouse
   e) Here is their new address 2 Buckingham Palace Road
   f) The teacher said its time you were going to lunch

2 Write out the sentences again using punctuation other than a colon. What could you use? Do you have to change the punctuation or add new words, such as conjunctions?

WORD

1 Look up and write the meanings of these connective words.
   therefore   notwithstanding   however   nevertheless   furthermore   though

2 Write them in sentences to show their meanings.

3 *a)* Write out the words, breaking them down into syllables.
   b) Circle the prefixes and suffixes and underline the root words to notice how they are spelled.

4 Use the *Look, say, cover, write, check* method to learn the words.

Writing a playscript

1 Read the passage from *The Wind in the Willows* (page 20) again. Copy this chart and find evidence to complete it.

What makes a playscript?	
Characters' names are written on the left	
Names start a new line when they speak	
There are no speech marks	
There is no use of 'he said', etc.	
Stage directions are used for actions, and are written in italics	
Prompts to actors appear in brackets	

2 Write the information you are given about the life of Anne Frank in *Anne Frank Beyond the Diary* (page 26) as a play, using all these features.

3 Create a playscript from the writings of Henry Mayhew in *Penny for the Guy* (page 28). Make sure that the words, expressions and reactions you give the characters suit Victorian times.

Being a journalist

4 Read the story from *The Wind in the Willows* (page 20) and imagine it in a more modern setting. Write a newspaper article about it.

Produce a copy and redraft it, using a word processor, where possible, so you can experiment with layout and typefaces. Now publish it.

Biography

5 Re-read *Anne Frank Beyond the Diary* (page 26) to revise the characteristics of a biography. You will notice that it is generally written in the third person and the past tense, e.g. Anne Frank lived in Amsterdam.

6 Write David's story from *I am David* (page 22) or Adrian Mole's story from *The Secret Diary of Adrian Mole Aged Thirteen and Three Quarters* (page 24) as if you were writing a biography. Use the information you are given in the passage, but use your imagination to think about what might happen to the characters later.

7 Choose a famous person about whom you would like to find out more, e.g. Mother Teresa of Calcutta, and do some research about his or her life. Use reference books and CD-ROMs. When you have enough details about the kind of person he or she was, write the first chapter of the biography. Check the details you use to make sure it is accurate.

Handy hints on making a class newspaper

Planning

What kind of newspaper will it be?

Who will be the editor?

What will go in it – fashion, sport, music, news?
Who will write the articles?

Writing

Who will be the audience for the article?

What should it look like?

What about the pictures?

Editing

Look at each other's work. Can it be improved?

Is it what a newspaper article should be like?

Putting it together

Which pieces will go in the newspaper?

How will the newspaper be printed?

How will you make it look attractive?

Final version

Who will proofread the articles?

What will the front page be like?

How will it be printed?

Will it be sold or given away?

How will you get feedback from your readers?

How are you getting on with the skills in the chart? If you need extra practice, try the numbered activities.

Grammar and punctuation	Verbs and tenses	1
	Active and passive verbs	2
	Semi-colons	3
	Colons	4
Spelling, phonics and vocabulary	Suffixes	5
	Origins of names	6
	Etymological dictionaries	7
	Mnemonics	8
	Spelling connectives	9

1 *a)* Rewrite this passage changing all the verbs to the past tense:

The fish rise to the surface and grab their food. Afterwards they vanish into the water. I find it difficult to leave the beautiful scene. However I take the hook off the fishing rod and pack away the gear. I feel happy that there is such a place to fish. I shove off in my boat and paddle to the shore as the fish swim away.

b) Underline all the verbs. Explain what changes have taken place.

2 Rewrite these sentences by changing the verbs from the active to the passive form or from the passive to the active form:

The litter was collected by the cleaners. My sister threw her plate out of the window. Class 7 put on an exhibition of their artwork. The store was crowded with shoppers. The ball was kicked into the net by the goalie. Our teacher told the class to be quiet.

3 *a)* Rewrite these sentences putting in the semi-colons:

The right of the class contained seven desks the left-hand side was empty now.

She slept quietly in the back of the car her father drove on.

Bring me apple pie and cream some sticky toffee puddings with custard all over them chocolate biscuits made in the old-fashioned way.

The disco was deserted only one couple moved slowly to the music.

b) Explain why you used the semi-colons where you did.

4 *a)* Rewrite these sentences putting in the colons:

You will need the following two eggs, half a kilogram of flour and some butter.

You take that road I'll take this road.

Only one thing would make him happy revenge.

She had not done her homework again she would get into trouble.

b) Explain why you used the colons where you did.

5 *a)* For each of these suffixes, write an example of a word that ends in this way: able, er, est, ful, tion, or, less.

b) Use the words in sentences to show their meanings.

c) Explain how adding the suffix changes the spelling of the root word, if it does.

6 *a)* Which of the surnames is the odd one out in each case? Give reasons for your answers:

Field, Bush, Smith, Hill; O'Neill, Fitzpatrick, MacDonald, Baker; Painter, Johnson, Baker, Smith.

b) Look carefully at these surnames. Explain where they are derived from: Clark, Townsend, Ford, Redhead, Tanner.

7 *a)* Find out the derivation and origin of these words:

boomerang   sherbet   barbecue   potato   plunder polka

b) Sort these words into three columns of French, Italian and Indian words. Use a dictionary to help you check which column they should go in.

disco   opera   studio   bungalow   veranda   cinema vanilla   shampoo   dessert

8 Write some mnemonics to help you to remember how to spell these words. Look at the clues in brackets: listen (list); what (hat); teacher (ache); elephant (ant).

9 Write down these words and circle two separate words within them, e.g. there - fore: however, furthermore.

Handy hints for spelling

◆ Is the word spelt as it sounds? Does it contain any phonemes you already know?

◆ Does the word look right? Do you know any other words like it?

◆ Can you break the word into smaller parts? Which is the most difficult part of the word?

◆ Do you know what the word means?

◆ Have you used a word book or dictionary to help you?

The Iron Man

The Iron Man has appeared in the countryside and is causing havoc, eating everything metal he can find. The local farmers have to think of a way to stop him.

The Iron Man stood up straight. Slowly he turned, till he was looking directly at Hogarth.

"We're sorry we trapped you and buried you," shouted the little boy. "We promise we'll not deceive you again. Follow us and you can have all the metal you want. Brass too. Aluminium too. And lots of old chrome. Follow us."

The Iron Man pushed aside the boughs and came into the lane, Hogarth joined the farmers. Slowly they drove back down the lane, and slowly, with all his cogs humming, the Iron Man stepped after them.

They led through the villages. Half the people came out to stare, half ran to shut themselves inside bedrooms and kitchens. Nobody could believe their eyes when they saw the Iron Man marching behind the farmers.

At last they came to the town, and there was a great scrap-metal yard. Everything was there, old cars by the hundred, old trucks, old railway engines, old stoves, old refrigerators, old springs, bedsteads, bicycles, girders, gates, pans – all the scrap iron of the region was piled up there, rusting away.

"There," cried Hogarth.
"Eat all you can."

The Iron Man gazed, and his eyes turned red. He kneeled down in the yard, he stretched out on one elbow. He picked up a greasy black stove and chewed on it. He followed that with a double-decker bedstead and the brass knobs made his eyes crackle with joy. Never before had the Iron Man eaten such delicacies. As he lay there, a big truck turned into the yard and unloaded a pile of rusty chain. The Iron Man lifted a handful and let it dangle into his mouth – better than any spaghetti.

So there they left him. It was an Iron Man's heaven. The farmers went back to their farms. Hogarth visited the Iron Man every few days. Now the Iron Man's eyes were constantly a happy blue. He was no longer rusty. His body gleamed blue, like a new gun barrel. And he ate, ate, ate, ate – endlessly.

Ted Hughes

TEXT

1 *a)* What two things was the boy sorry for?

b) What did he promise not to do again?

2 *a)* As the Iron Man and the men walked through the village, why do you think the people came out to stare? *b)* How else did they react? *c)* What does this indicate about how they felt?

3 *a)* List five things in the scrap-metal yard that would please the Iron Man.

b) Why do you think he would be happy?

4 Describe how the Iron Man reacted to the scrap-metal yard.

5 Quote some words from the passage to show that the Iron Man saw the metal objects as food.

6 *a)* Explain how you felt about the Iron Man at the beginning of the passage.

b) How did you feel about him at the end? How was this different?

SENTENCE

1 Copy this passage, changing all the verbs into the passive.

My mum weighed some flour and broke some eggs into a bowl. She creamed the butter with the sugar until it was light. She then combined all the ingredients and mixed them. Finally she put the cake to bake in the oven.

2 Copy this passage, changing all the verbs into the active.

An electric plug was taken by my mum. A screwdriver was placed in the back of the plug. The screw attaching the two plastic pieces was removed. The brown wire was connected to the right terminal. The blue wire was connected to the left terminal. The earth wire was connected to the terminal at the top. The two pieces of the plug were joined together again and the plug was tested.

WORD

1 From which one country do these words or expressions come?

au revoir   café   menu   encore   fiancée   hors d'oeuvre   au pair

2 Write the words in sentences to show what they mean.

3 Find out where these words come from.

ballet   depot   cabaret   bouquet   croquet   parquet

Look at the word endings. How can this help you to learn to spell them?

4 From which language do these words or expressions come? What do they mean?

post mortem   post meridian   vice versa   anno domini

5 From which countries do these words come?

siesta   karate   anorak   chocolate   opera

6 Write the words in sentences to show what they mean.

Colonel Fazackerley

Colonel Fazackerley's house is haunted, but the ghost has a harder time scaring him than usual.

Colonel Fazackerley Butterworth-Toast
Bought an old castle complete with a ghost,
But someone or other forgot to declare
To Colonel Fazackerley that the spectre was there.

On the very first evening, while waiting to dine,
The Colonel was taking a fine sherry wine,
When the ghost, with a furious flash and a flare
Shot out of the chimney and shivered, "Beware!"

Colonel Fazackerley put down his glass
And said, "My dear fellow, that's really first class!
I just can't conceive how you do it all at all.
I imagine you're going to a Fancy Dress Ball?"

At this, the dread ghost gave a withering cry.
Said the Colonel (his monocle firm in his eye),
"Now just how you do it I wish I could think.
Do sit down and tell me, and please have a drink."

The ghost in his phosphorous cloak gave a roar
And floated about between ceiling and floor.
He walked through a wall and returned through a pane
And backed up the chimney and came down again.

Said the Colonel, "With laughter I'm feeling quite weak!"
(As trickles of merriment ran down his cheek).
"My house-warming party I hope you won't spurn.
You *must* say you'll come and you'll give us a turn!"

At this, the poor spectre – quite out of his wits –
Proceeded to shake himself almost to bits.
He rattled his chains and he clattered his bones
And he filled the whole castle with mumbles and moans.

But Colonel Fazackerley, just as before,
Was simply delighted and called out, "Encore!"
At which the ghost vanished, his efforts in vain,
And never was seen at the castle again.

"Oh dear, what a pity!" said the Colonel Fazack,
"I don't know his name, so I can't call him back."
And then with a smile that was hard to define,
Colonel Fazackerley went in to dine.

Charles Causley

TEXT

1 What other word is used to mean 'ghost' in the first verse?

2 *a)* Explain what the Colonel thinks the ghost is doing when he first sees it.
b) Why should he think this?

3 Look in a dictionary and write what these words from the poem mean.
monocle phosphorous merriment withering

4 *a)* How do we know that the Colonel finds the ghost amusing?
b) What does he ask him to do at his next party?

5 *a)* Explain why the ghost leaves.
b) What do the last two lines of the poem say about the Colonel's part in this?

6 What do you find amusing in this poem and why? Write under three sub-headings: words and expressions, people and their description, the events.

SENTENCE

1 Reorder and join these groups of simple sentences to make one, longer and more interesting sentence each time. The connectives in brackets provide suggestions. You do not have to use them all.

a) He made coffee. He walked along the beach. He was waiting for the sunset. (after, because, before)

b) The day was hot. The beach was quiet. Fred could not think about returning. (however, and, but, so, therefore)

c) It was quiet. She felt something move. She thought she was being watched. (suddenly, and, nevertheless, although)

d) The Colonel saw the ghost. He laughed. He would get rid of it. It would be a challenge. (eventually, so, and, however, even though, despite the fact that)

WORD

1 Write out these words and circle the final letter.
lone scarce approximate intense precise severe fortunate
Which end in a vowel and which a consonant?

2 Now add 'ly' to the words. Does anything happen to the final letter of the word? Check your spelling in a dictionary.

3 Add 'ful', 'ment' or 'less' to ten words. *a)* Do these suffixes begin with a vowel or a consonant? *b)* Does anything happen to the final letter of the word? Check your spelling in a dictionary.

4 Can you form a rule about adding suffixes to words ending in 'e'?

5 Find out what happens with the spelling of the following when you add suffixes.
probable possible true argue whole nine

The Sword in the Stone

Merlyn the Magician and Madame Mim have a competition of magic where tactics is all.

Merlyn and Madame Mim rolled up their sleeves, gave their surcoats to Hecate to hold and the latter put on a celluloid eye-shade to watch the battle.

At the first gong Madame Mim immediately turned herself into a dragon. It was the accepted opening move and Merlyn ought to have replied by being a thunderstorm or something like that. Instead he caused a great deal of preliminary confusion by becoming a field mouse, which was quite invisible in the grass, and nibbled Madame Mim's tail, as she stared about in all directions, for about five minutes before she noticed him. But when she did notice the nibbling, she was a furious cat in two flicks.

Wart held his breath to see what the mouse would become next – he thought perhaps a tiger which could kill the cat – but Merlyn merely became another cat. He stood opposite her and made faces. This most irregular procedure put Madame Mim quite out of her stride, and it took her more than a minute to regain her bearings and become a dog. Even as she became it, Merlyn was another dog standing opposite her, of the same sort.

"Oh, well played, sir!" cried the Wart, beginning to see the plan.

Madame Mim was furious. She felt herself out of her depth against the unusual stone-walling tactics and experienced an internal struggle not to lose her temper. She knew that if she did lose it she would lose her judgement, and the battle as well. She did some quick thinking. If whenever she turned herself into a menacing animal, Merlyn was merely going to turn into the same kind, the thing would become either a mere dog-fight or a stalemate. She had better alter her own tactics and give Merlyn a surprise.

At this moment the gong went for the end of the first round. The combatants retired into their respective corners and their seconds cooled them by flapping their wings, while Archimedes gave Merlyn a little massage by nibbling with his beak.

"Second round," commanded Hecate. "Seconds out of the ring … Time!"

Clang went the gong, and the two desperate wizards stood face to face.

T. H. White

TEXT

1 *a)* What did Madame Mim turn herself into at first? *b)* How did Merlyn retaliate?

2 *a)* Why was this a surprise to the spectators? *b)* How did Madame Mim react?

3 *a)* Why did Wart think Merlyn would turn into a tiger?
b) Explain what Merlin did turn himself into and why this was a clever move.

4 Why do you think Madame Mim was angry? Give your reasons.

5 Write about why Madame Mim decided to 'change her tactics'.

6 Write the words from the passage that suggest the writer is comparing this magic competition to a boxing match.

7 The competition is described stage by stage. Write a sentence to show what happens in every paragraph.

SENTENCE

1 Match statements from Column A to clauses in Column B, to make interesting sentences.

A Statement with verb	B Clause
Merlyn met Madame Mim	but continued after a break
Madame Mim changed into a cat	when Merlyn changed into a nasty germ
The competition ended	who wanted to fight
It all ended later	which ate a mouse

2 Add a clause of your own to make these sentences more interesting. Use 'because', 'or', 'if', 'as'.

a) He watched the game. *b)* Merlyn will not be pleased. *c)* The competition ended in a draw. *d)* She did not like to be defeated. *e)* He will win the magic competition.

WORD

1 Explain what these proverbs mean: 'Too many cooks spoil the broth', 'Many hands make light work', 'When the cat's away the mice will play'.

2 Match up the two halves of these proverbs and write them out.

Never judge a	is better than none
Do not cut off your nose	before you leap
Look	to spite your face
Half a loaf	book by its cover

3 Put all the proverbs into sentences to show their meaning.

Facts on Alcohol

Drinking and Driving

In Britain, alcohol-related road accidents are the commonest cause of death in young men. People who drink and drive are not only being stupid with their own lives, they are selfishly endangering others. Passengers or pedestrians may also be killed or crippled for life.

There is no excuse for drinking and driving. Government advertising hammers the message home – 'save lives, don't drink and drive'.

With a little planning, everyone can avoid mixing alcohol and driving. Friends can club together to take a taxi. Or they can take it in turns to have a night off. They might even find that they enjoy themselves just as much.

It is against the law to drive with more than a certain level of alcohol in the blood. People who do are said to be 'over the limit'. The limit is very low, and even one drink can put you over.

The same rules apply to bicycling and swimming – 'don't do it after drinking'.

The Breathalyser

After you have had an alcoholic drink, there is alcohol on your breath, and in your blood and urine. In most countries it is illegal to drive a motor vehicle with more than a certain amount of alcohol in the bloodstream. Police often use a breathalyser to measure the alcohol in the breath and to check if a driver is over the limit. If so, the driver is usually taken to a police station for a more accurate test to be made on urine or blood.

Consequences

Being drunk is no excuse for committing a crime. In fact drunkenness itself is generally against the law. Courts have little sympathy with people who fight, steal or cause damage while under the influence of alcohol. Violent hooligans receive severe punishments. Under-age drinking often leads to an unpleasant encounter with the police. Getting a criminal record is not a sensible way to start life. People who are caught drinking and driving usually lose their driving licence. This can badly affect people's lives. Some people could lose their jobs if this happened.

Statistics

Many car accidents are related to drinking, which is why there are laws about drinking and driving. Many offenders are young people.

> **US: 17 per cent of all drink and drive offences due to 18-20 year-olds**
>
> **UK: 33 per cent of all drink and drive offenders are under 25**

TEXT

1 What does the passage say is the commonest cause of death in young men?

2 Find two words in the second sentence that show the author's attitude to this.

3 What is a breathalyser? What does it do? How do you think it might prevent people from drinking and driving?

4 Write three consequences of drinking and driving.

5 *a)* Why do the statistics about drinking and driving in the United Kingdom show that this is a serious problem? *b)* Explain why the statistics from the United States are given to you as a comparison.

6 Write a paragraph about how the writer persuades you with his argument. Consider the use of sub-headings, diagrams to make things clearer, information in boxes and examples.

SENTENCE

1 These words and phrases often appear on official documents. Use a dictionary to suggest words you might use instead.

forename occupation institution marital status duplicate applicant current maiden name nationality block letters

2 Design an application form for joining a club you know, using your own words. What information do you need? Now use the official words and phrases. Which form is better and why?

3 Official documents are often written in the second person – you. Explain why these documents do not use the first person – I, or the third person – he/she/they.

4 *a)* Rewrite your school rules using personal pronouns, e.g. you, we, I, and remove any official-sounding words or phrases.
   b) What differences do you notice? Should rules be written in an official or unofficial way?

WORD

1 Write out these words, putting the number of syllables they contain in brackets, e.g. trying (2).

returning altogether dreadful pencil gymnastics catalogue shall

2 Divide these words into syllables and write them out. Explain how dividing them into syllables helps you spell the tricky double letter.

saddle kettle middle scribble bottle bubble puzzle

3 These words all contain a vowel that often gets missed out in spelling. Write them out. Divide them into syllables and circle the letter that often gets left out.

interest extraordinary carpet poisonous

4 Use the *Look, say, cover, write, check* method to learn all the words in this section.

Moonfleet

It is the 1700s. John Trenchard is trapped in the vaults of the church, hiding from smugglers. When they leave, he tries to make his escape.

Thus, sitting where I was, I lit my candle once more, and then clambered across that great coffin which, for two hours or more, had been a mid-wall of partition between me and danger. But to get out of the niche was harder than to get in; for now that I had a candle to light me, I saw that the coffin, though sound enough to outer view, was wormed through and through, and little better than a rotten shell. So it was that I had some ado to get over it, not daring either to kneel upon it or to bring much weight to bear with my hand, lest it should go through. And now having got safely across, I sat for an instant on that narrow ledge of the stone shelf which projected beyond the coffin on the vault side, and made ready to jump forward onto the floor below. And how it happened I know not, but there I lost my balance, and as I slipped the candle flew out of my grasp. Then I clutched at the coffin to save myself, but my hand went clean through it, and so I came to the ground in a cloud of dust and splinters; having only got hold of a wisp of seaweed, or a handful of those draggled funeral trappings which were strewn about this place. The floor of the vault was sandy; and so, though I fell crookedly, I took but little harm beyond the shaking; and soon, pulling

myself together, set to strike my flint and blow the match into a flame to search for the fallen candle. Yet all the time I kept in my fingers this handful of light stuff; and when the flame burnt up again I held the thing against the light, and saw that it was no wisp of seaweed, but something black and wiry. For a moment, I could not gather what I had hold of, but then gave a start that nearly sent the candle out, and perhaps a cry, and let it drop as if it were red-hot iron, for I knew that it was a man's beard.

Now when I saw that, I felt a sort of throttling fright, as though one had caught hold of my heartstrings; and so many and such strange thoughts rose in me, that the blood went pounding round and round in my head, as it did once afterwards when I was fighting with the sea and near drowned. Surely to have in hand the beard of any dead man in any place was bad enough, but worse a thousand times in such a place as this, and to know on whose face it had grown. For, almost before I fully saw what it was, I knew it was that black beard which had given Colonel John Mohune his nickname, and that was his coffin I had hid behind.

J. Meade Faulkner

TEXT

1 *a)* What had John (the subject of the extract) been hiding behind in the vault?
b) How long had he been there?

2 *a)* What happened just as he was going to jump on the floor?
b) What did he do to save himself?

3 *a)* What did John think he had grasped? *b)* What did it turn out to be?
c) How did John react?

4 *a)* Why do you think John was not hurt when he fell?
b) What did he do when he 'pulled himself together'?

5 To what experience does John compare his fear?

6 Write a paragraph about how we know this novel is set in the past. Find examples of the words used and the details and events mentioned.

SENTENCE

1 Add a sentence to the beginning of these 'because' clauses to make an interesting sentence. *a)* because I was hot. *b)* because she left early. *c)* because they asked for a computer. *d)* because it never worked.

2 Add a sentence to the beginning of these 'when' clauses to make an interesting sentence. *a)* when I have grown up. *b)* when it happened. *c)* when the sunset faded into the sea. *d)* when Mum dropped the cream cake on his head.

3 Copy these sentences but add a clause. *a)* Glen loved to eat chocolate, though…
b) The garden shed fell down in the wind although…
c) The concert was cancelled although…

WORD

1 Use a dictionary to collect ten words beginning with 'bi', e.g. bicycle. Show how you can use a prefix to work out what a word means.

2 *a)* Look up these words in a dictionary. Write the shortest, simplest word that means the same.

   commence   endeavour   imbibe   expedite   persist

b) Now look up the same words in a thesaurus. Find two other words that mean the same.

3 Dictionaries can help you to pronounce words correctly.
a) Write some notes to explain how to pronounce these words.

   advertisement   lieutenant   infamous   courtesy   gauge

b) Write down their meanings.

Using the text as a model

1 Look at how Charles Causley (page 36) uses the ballad form of the poem to make his subject funny.

rhyming in couplets

> At **this,** the poor **spec**tre – quite **out** of his **wits** –
> Pro**ceed**ed to **shake** himself **al**most to **bits**.
> He **rat**tled his **chains** and he **clat**tered his **bones**
> And he **filled** the whole **cas**tle with **mum**bles and **moans**.

four lines in a verse

rhythm of the lines – four strong beats

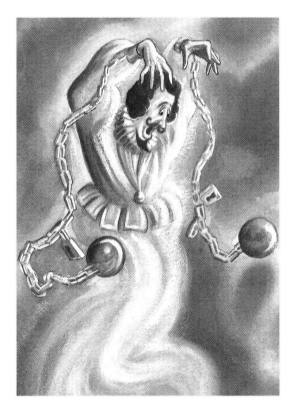

Write two more verses for the poem in which the ghost tries to frighten the Colonel, who is cleverly pretending it is all a joke.

◆ Use the same pattern as in the example.

◆ Imagine some amusing tricks by the ghost.

◆ Use expressions from speech, e.g. 'almost to bits… out of his wits… '

You could start:

'He poked round the corner, his head in his hands… '

or

'The ghost floated round him, his feet in the air… '

Write the ghost's diary using the events in the poem. Was it so funny for him?

◆ Make a list of the events in the poem – what happened and the results.

◆ Describe what happened to you (as the ghost) and how you felt about it.

Using different genres for ideas

2 Continue with the story of *Moonfleet* (page 42).

◆ What happens to John in the vault?

◆ What happens as he tries to escape from it?

◆ What happens when he does find his way out?

Remember:

This is a story set in the 1700s. Try to use the correct words from the time, e.g. 'thus', 'so it was that', etc. Use the correct detail from the time, e.g. striking a flint to light a candle.

3 *The Sword in the Stone* (page 38) is written in the style of a fantasy novel. Write the first chapter of your own fantasy novel containing magicians, magic swords, a lost king and a battle between magicians.

Remember:

Fantasy can contain anything – it does not have to stick to the historical time, or it can be amusing. Do not spend too long telling your reader the detail – make people like your characters through their speech as well.

Writing an argument

4 Write an article for a newspaper arguing that the *Iron Man* (page 34) is a nuisance to society and should be removed immediately from the scrap yard.

Remember:

Write in the style of a newspaper, following the rules in the Handy hints for writing an argument checklist. What evidence do you have? Is the Iron Man doing some good? Is he just frightening people into being nice to him? Does he deserve to be given this treat?

Handy hints for writing an argument

Topic

Is it something you know about?

◆ do you know what are the facts?
◆ have you given your reader false information?
◆ have you stated your opinion as if it were fact?

Logic

Is what you are saying logical?

◆ have you started with a plan?
◆ do you know everything you will say?
◆ have you reached a conclusion?
◆ is your argument easy to follow?

Acceptability

Is what you are saying acceptable to your reader?

◆ are you prejudiced?
◆ do you only give one side of the argument?
◆ have you backed up your argument with examples?

Flow

◆ have you used words and phrases which will develop your argument, e.g. 'therefore', 'consequently', 'as a result', 'obviously'?
◆ have you used words and phrases which will move your argument forwards, e.g. 'but', 'alternatively', 'however', 'nevertheless'?

How are you getting on with the things in the chart? If you need extra practice try the activities shown.

Grammar and punctuation	Active and passive verbs	1
	Making complex sentences	2
	Revision of clauses	3
	Official language	4
	Connecting clauses	5
Spelling, phonics and vocabulary	Word origins and derivation	6
	Spelling rules – dropping the 'e'	7
	Proverbs	8
	Revision of spelling by syllables	9

1 *a)* Copy this passage, changing all the verbs into the passive.

The dog dragged the boy up the hill. His teacher met him and spoke to him. When he arrived home his mum told him off for being late.

b) Copy this passage changing all the verbs into the active.

The football match was taking place on Saturday. All the team were driven there by my father. They were singing in the back of the car.

2 Write out each of these groups of simple sentences to make one longer, more interesting sentence each time.

a) It was raining. The girl went out. It was five o'clock. She carried her new umbrella. (although, when, because, since)

b) The tree in my garden is to be chopped down. It is very old. It is not safe. I am sad. It is urgent. (because, although, unless, which, that, while)

3 Add a clause of your own to make these sentences more interesting. Use 'although', 'or', 'until' and 'as'.

You will have to wait. Mum stood with her arms folded. She was determined to win. Dad still burned his hand. I refused to take my umbrella.

4 Make these official-sounding sentences easy to understand, using a dictionary for help.

a) Personnel are requested to maintain due vigilance during experimental activities.

b) Vehicular travel should be excluded from areas primarily intended for pedestrian use.

5 Copy these sentences and add a clause.

a) I could not understand how…

b) I tripped over the rock which…

Now write ten new sentences using these words to join sentences and clauses together.

whether   when   though   until   which

6 *a)* Use your dictionary to find the meaning and origins of these words.

monorail   subterranean   transistor antibiotic

7 *a)* Add an 'e' to these words and describe what happens.

mat   fat   pip   win   bit   not   cub   plum

b) What happens when you add a suffix to a vowel, e.g. 'ing' to the following words?

place   guide   create   hope   bore

8 Rewrite these proverbs and metaphorical expressions to explain what they really mean.

a) I'm in a real jam.

b) That's a load of rubbish.

c) Put your shoulders to the wheel and we'll make it happen.

d) He was so guilty, his face was a picture.

9 *a)* Write out these words and divide them into syllables.

operation   invitation   examination   competition

Explain how dividing the words into syllables can help you to spell tricky endings.

b) Write out these words and divide them into syllables. Circle the letter that often gets left out.

freedom   terrific   description   company   portable

Handy hints for spelling

◆ Is the word spelt as it sounds? Does it contain any phonemes you already know?

◆ Does the word look right? Do you know any other words like it?

◆ Can you break the word into smaller parts? Which is the most difficult part of the word?

◆ Do you know what the word means?

◆ Have you used a word book or dictionary to help you?

LOOK   SAY   COVER   WRITE   CHECK

The War of the Worlds

The writer is watching as an alien, which has just landed on Earth, comes out of its spacecraft.

The end of the cylinder was being screwed out from within. Nearly two feet of shining screw projected. Somebody blundered against me, and I narrowly missed being pitched onto the top of the screw. I turned, and as I did so the screw must have come out, and the lid of the cylinder fell upon the gravel with a ringing concussion. I stuck my elbow into the person behind me and turned my head towards the Thing again. For a moment that circular cavity seemed perfectly black. I had the sunset in my eyes.

I think everyone expected to see a man emerge – possibly something a little unlike us terrestrial men, but in all essentials a man. I know I did. But, looking, I presently saw something stirring within the shadow – greyish billowy movements, one above another, and then two luminous discs like eyes. Then something resembling a little grey snake, about the thickness of a walking-stick, coiled up out of the writhing middle, and wriggled in the air towards me – and then another.

A sudden chill came over me. There was a loud shriek from a woman behind.

I half turned, keeping my eyes fixed upon the cylinder still, from which other tentacles were now projecting, and began pushing my way back from the edge of the pit. I found myself alone, and saw the people on the other side of the pit running off … I looked again at the cylinder, and ungovernable terror gripped me. I stood petrified and staring.

A big, greyish, rounded bulk, the size perhaps of a bear, was rising slowly and painfully out of the cylinder. As it bulged up and caught the light, it glistened like wet leather. Two large dark-coloured eyes were regarding me steadfastly. It was rounded, and had, one might say, a face. There was a mouth under the eyes, the lipless rim of which quivered and panted, and dropped saliva. The body heaved and pulsated convulsively. A lank tentacular appendage gripped the edge of the cylinder, another swayed in the air.

H. G. Wells

TEXT

1 How did the writer know that the lid of the cylinder had fallen on to the ground?

2 Explain why the writer could not see what was in the cylinder at first.

3 *a)* What did people expect to come out of the cylinder?
b) Describe what the author first saw.

4 *a)* Describe the reaction of the crowd when the alien came out.
b) Explain why the author was left by himself.
c) Would you have reacted in the same way? Give your reasons.

5 Use a dictionary to write the meanings of these words as they are used in the passage.
pulsated   convulsively   tentacular   appendage

6 Write a paragraph about how the author builds up suspense slowly. Write a sentence to describe what is happening in each paragraph.

SENTENCE

1 One way to summarise is to write sentences as newspaper headlines, e.g. 'Two women were killed yesterday when their car hit a lorry on the M1' could become 'Two women killed – car hits lorry on M1'. Write headlines for the following.

a) The staff meeting started at four o'clock in the afternoon.
b) Reptiles can be defined as cold-blooded animals which lay eggs.
c) The Second World War lasted from 1939 right through to the middle of 1945.

2 *a)* Read the passage below. Write down, the four symptoms of measles.

Doctors tell us there are obvious symptoms of measles. The first is a sore throat and then the patient suffers from a raging temperature. After this the many spots break out all over the body. Soon after the poor patient feels exhausted and must rest.

WORD

1 *a)* Copy these words and circle the 'ie' or 'ei'.

chief   ceiling   yield   deceive   receive   receipt   priest   believe   piece   perceive

2 *a)* Write down the sound that the 'ie' or 'ei' makes by writing a word that rhymes with it.
b) Underline the letter that comes before the 'ie' or 'ei'.
c) Write a rule about when 'ie' and 'ei' should be used.

3 Write these words.
Neil   seize   protein   Sheila   Keith

Circle the 'ie' or 'ei' sound. Do they follow your rule or are they exceptions?

4 Find ten more 'ie' or 'ei' words, e.g. friend. Do they follow your rule? If so, why?

The Eagle of the Ninth

This extract is set in Ancient Britain, during the Roman occupation. Marcus, a Roman, has sent his servant to buy a slave. Marcus has already saved the slave's life.

Marcus waited for their return alone in the atrium, for Uncle Aquila had retired to his watch-tower study to work out a particularly absorbing problem in siege warfare. He had been trying to read his uncle's copy of the Georgics, but his thoughts kept wandering from Virgil on bee-keeping to the encounter before him. He was wondering for the first time – he had not thought to wonder before – why the fate of a slave gladiator he had never before set eyes on should matter to him so dearly. But it did matter. Maybe it was like calling to like; and yet it was hard to see quite what he had in common with a barbarian slave.

Presently his listening ear caught the sound of an arrival in the slaves' quarters, and he laid down the papyrus roll and turned toward the doorway. Steps came along the colonnade, and two figures appeared on the threshold. "Centurion Marcus, I have brought the new slave," said Stephanos, and stepped discreetly back into the night; and the new slave walked forward to the foot of Marcus's couch, and stood there.

For a long moment the two young men looked at each other, alone in the empty lamplit atrium as yesterday they had been alone in the crowded amphitheatre, while the scuff-scuffling of Stephanos's sandals died away down from the colonnade.

"So it is you," the slave said at last.

"Yes, it is I."

The silence began again, and again the slave broke it. "Why did you turn the purpose of the crowd yesterday? I did not ask for mercy."

"Possibly that was why."

The slave hesitated, and then said defiantly, "I was afraid yesterday; I, who have been a warrior. I am afraid to choke out my life in the Fisher's net."

"I know," Marcus said. "But still, you did not ask for mercy." The other's eyes were fixed on his face, a little puzzled. "Why have you bought me?"

Rosemary Sutcliff

TEXT

1 *a)* Where was Marcus waiting? Look in a dictionary if you are unsure about the meaning of the word. *b)* Where had his uncle gone?

2 *a)* What was the name of Marcus' servant?
   b) Find some evidence to show that he treated Marcus as his master.

3 How do we know that Marcus is an officer in the Roman army?

4 Write down the evidence that tells us that Marcus had saved the new slave's life.

5 *a)* Why do you think the new slave was puzzled?
   b) What words in the passage show that he is not accustomed to being a slave?

6 This passage comes from a historical novel. Write down the words the writer uses to do with ancient Rome, its buildings, its sports, its books and writers. Look in a dictionary to find their meanings.

SENTENCE

1 Copy the sentences and underline the conditional verbs.

   a) I should be grateful if you would return my coat. *b)* We would go if we could afford it. *c)* My mother should be able to come if she gets better. *d)* Dad would not watch the match even though he had a ticket. *e)* You should go to bed if you feel sleepy.
   f) Could I borrow your book if I promised to return it?

2 Which three words do you notice are usually used to show the conditional?

3 Which words in the sentences show that the actions depend on something or somebody else and are not certain?

4 Write five more sentences using these conditionals and underline the conditional verbs.

WORD

1 Write sentences to show how words within words can help you to remember how to spell these words, e.g. elephant (ant) – an ant is small and an elephant is huge.

   temperature (temper)   practise (is)   money (one)   chocolate (ate)   listener (list)

2 Invent some mnemonics which could help you to spell 'the' words.

   then   there   them   they   their   there

   Write sentences using these words to show you know the difference in their meanings.

3 Try to find the answers to these riddles, e.g. 'Which is the friendliest colour?'
   'White – because it says Hi'. *a)* Why is the letter U always happy? (think of fun)
   b) How can words become dangerous when you add a letter W?
   c) Which word is the longest and happiest in the world? (think of a mile and an S)

Water Supplies

Water is vital to support life, but is it easily available everywhere?

Water

Each year about 5 million people die from inadequate water supplies and sanitation.

If you look at the Earth from space, water appears to be in plentiful supply – it covers 70 per cent of the planet's surface. However, water in the oceans and seas is salty and cannot be used in agriculture, for industry or by people until it has been treated.

Only about three per cent of the world's water is fresh and most of that is locked up in the polar ice caps. The remainder is spread out very unevenly across the Earth's surface. The Great Lakes of North America alone hold 18 per cent of the world's fresh water. Water use is also spread unevenly – the average person in the USA uses over 300 litres of water per day compared with less than 6 litres per day in Madagascar. In the UK, the figure is 150 litres per person per day.

Using water

Water is essential for producing food, and is also used in many industries. More importantly than these uses, however, it sustains human and animal life. Without water a person can only survive for a few days. Our bodies are largely made up of water – 90 per cent when measured by volume, and 66 per cent when measured by weight.

Apart from drinking, water is also used for:

- food preparation and cooking
- personal hygiene and washing clothes
- waste disposal
- agriculture
- industrial production
- power generation
- transportation
- recreation.

Safe water

The quality of water used by people is vitally important as contaminated water combined with inadequate sanitation (e.g. poor drainage and sewage removal) contribute to a range of diseases. In an attempt to combat this the United Nations designated 1981–90 the International Drinking Water Supply and Sanitation Decade. During this period approximately 535 million people gained access to safe water supplies, and 325 million people received adequate sanitation facilities. For some countries the impact was dramatic. In Burkina Faso the percentage of the population having access to clean water rose from 30 to 68 per cent. Despite successes such as this, one in five of the world's population are still without a satisfactory water supply and almost half lack adequate sanitation.

Percentage of the population with access to safe water and sanitation

	safe water	sanitation water
Bangladesh	97	34
Brazil	87	83
Chile	85	83
China	67	24
India	81	29
Kenya	53	77
Mexico	83	50
Namibia	57	34

Global Eye

TEXT

1 How many people die every year from 'inadequate water supplies and sanitation'? Use a dictionary and write the meanings of 'inadequate' and 'sanitation'.

2 *a)* How much water covers the Earth's surface?   *b)* Why can we not use most of it?

3 Why is some of the water difficult to get at?

4 What evidence does the writer give to prove that 'water use is spread unevenly'?

5 List five important uses for water, besides drinking it.

6 *a)* Why do you think water is described as 'unsafe'?
 b) What did the United Nations do to give people 'safe water'?

7 Find examples from the passage of these features of a balanced argument: easy-to-understand statistics, examples to prove points, does not blame any one thing or person.

SENTENCE

1 Read the passage again.
 a) Write down the figures about water that you are given in each paragraph.
 b) How would you write the following in a shortened form?
   percentage   litre   three quarters   the United States of America   the United Nations

2 Copy these sentences. Write the word or phrase in italic in note form, e.g. electricity could be shortened to elec. *a)* The train arrived at *approximately* 12 o'clock.
 b) He gave me his *telephone number*. *c)* We live in the *twentieth century*.
 d) He owed me *one pound* plus the concert ticket.

3 Write out these sentences in as short a form as possible. *a)* Shakespeare lived from 1564 right up to 1616. *b)* The pop concert lasted from 7.00 p.m. until 11.00 p.m.

WORD

1 Add 'able' to these words. Use a dictionary to check your spelling.
 accept   understand   detest   laugh   change   fashion   love   notice

2 *a)* Underline the root word and circle the suffixes to the words from question 1.
 b) What do you notice about the root words? Do they change?

3 Copy these 'ible' words. **terrible   possible   visible   edible   audible**
 a) Remove the suffix 'ible'. What are you left with?
 b) What do you notice about what is left, compared to the 'able' words?

4 Write a rule about to which sort of words 'able' and 'ible' can be added.

5 Find five more 'able' words and five more 'ible' words to check if your rule is correct.

The Phantom Tollbooth

Milo and his dog find themselves in the Kingdom of Dictionopolis, from where all the words in the world come.

Overhead a large banner proclaimed:
WELCOME TO THE WORD MARKET
And, across the square, five very tall thin gentlemen regally dressed in silks and satins, plumed hats, and buckled shoes rushed up to the car, stopped short, mopped five brows, caught five breaths, unrolled five parchments, and began talking in turn.
"Greetings!"
"Salutations!"
"Welcome!"
"Good afternoon!"
"Hello!"
Milo nodded his head, and they went on, reading from their scrolls.
"By order of Azaz the Unabridged –"
"King of Dictionopolis –"
"Monarch of letters –"
"Emperor of phrases, sentences and miscellaneous figures of speech –"
"We offer you the hospitality of our kingdom,"
"Country,"
"Nation,"
"State,"
"Commonwealth,"
"Realm,"
"Empire,"
"Palatinate,"
"Principality."
"Do all those words mean the same thing?"
"Of course,"
"Certainly,"
"Precisely,"
"Exactly,"
"Yes," they replied in order.
"Well, then," said Milo, not understanding why each one said the same thing in a slightly different way, "wouldn't it be simpler to use just one? It would certainly make more sense."
"Nonsense,"
"Ridiculous,"
"Fantastic,"
"Absurd,"
"Bosh," they chorused again, and continued:
"We're not interested in making sense; it's not our job," scolded the first. "Besides," explained the second, "one word is as good as another – so why not use them all?"
"Then you don't have to choose which one is right," advised the third.
"Besides," sighed the fourth, "if one is right, then ten are ten times as right."
"Obviously you don't know who we are," sneered the fifth. And they presented themselves one by one as:
"The Duke of Definition."
"The Minister of Meaning."
"The Earl of Essence."
"The Count of Connotation."
"The Under-Secretary of Understanding."

Norton Juster

TEXT

1 Explain what is strange about the banner that Milo sees.

2 *a)* Describe how the five men are dressed. *b)* Who sent them to meet Milo?

3 The men all use synonyms. What words do they use instead of 'hello' and 'kingdom'?

4 *a)* What is Milo's reason for using just one word for something?
b) How do the five men argue against this?

5 What evidence is there in the passage that the five men work for the government of the country?

6 This passage is from a humorous novel. What do you find amusing about it?
Use these ideas to help. What is strange about the events in the story? What is strange about the use of words? Do the characters behave in a strange or amusing way?

SENTENCE

1 Copy these sentences, underlining the conditional.

a) The cat could be given food.   The cat should be given food.
The cat was given food.
b) She should pass her exams.   She will pass her exams.   She passed her exams.
c) I would give him my chocolate.   I will give him my chocolate.
I gave him my chocolate.

2 Explain how the meanings of these groups of sentences are different because of the different uses of the verbs.

WORD

1 The meanings of words change over time. Use a dictionary to match up these words with their original meanings.

Words	Original meanings
naughty nice meat vulgar humour	food ordinary a body fluid worth nothing precise

2 Write sentences to show how these words are used today.

3 Write sentences to show how these words are used today.

horrible ghastly wicked bad mouse trainer

4 Say what they used to (and still do) mean.

5 Use the *Look, say, cover, write, check* method to learn how to spell the new words.

Children at Work

What the law says

▼ Children are not allowed to work in any job if under 13 years of age.

▼ School children must be issued with a work permit before beginning work.

▼ There is a maximum number of hours that can be worked each week which varies in different counties/regions. Contact your education welfare officer for details.

▼ Children aged 13 and over can only work after 7 am and before 7 pm.

▼ On a school day they can only work for up to 2 hours.

Keeping yourself safe at work

▼ Make sure your employer gets a work permit for you from your education welfare office.

▼ Know what the safety rules are at work.

▼ Don't overdo it and injure yourself – young people aren't as strong as older people.

▼ Tell your parents where you are working and what you are doing.

▼ Carry an emergency contact number in case you have an accident at work.

Delivery rounds

If you are walking:

▼ wear fluorescent clothing and reflective armbands or belts – others will see you more easily especially in the dark

▼ keep to the pavement

▼ find the safest place to cross the road – use a pedestrian crossing or traffic island where possible

▼ beware of dogs – tell your employer if you think there is a dangerous dog on your round.

If you are on a bike:

▼ wear a cycle helmet – this will help protect your head from serious injury

▼ wear bright, reflective clothing like armbands and a belt

▼ make sure that your bike lights and reflectors are working

▼ keep your bike in good working order

▼ go on a cycling training course – contact your road safety officer for details.

Babysitting

There is no law about the age that you can babysit. But if anything happens to the children being looked after by someone under 16, the parents who employ the babysitter are legally responsible.

Babysitting is a big responsibility, so if you are under 16, think carefully about how confident you'd feel looking after young children.

▼ Have a contact telephone number for the parents and know what time they'll be back.

▼ Learn how safety equipment works, like stairgates and fireguards.

▼ Keep hot drinks, matches and lighters out of reach of babies and small children.

▼ Keep little children and little toys apart – they can choke on toys for older children.

Child Accident Prevention Trust

TEXT

1 *a)* When can children over 13 work? *b)* How many hours a day are they allowed to work?

2 What two pieces of advice does this document give children about work?

3 If you are riding a bike at work, what five things does this document advise you to do?

4 *a)* Why do you think babysitting is 'a big responsibility'?
b) If something happens to a baby you are looking after, who is responsible?

5 *a)* Why is it important for you to know about safety equipment, e.g. fireguards?
b) Write what other dangers are mentioned.

6 Find some evidence from the passage to show these features of an official document: subheadings, bullet points, short sentences, the imperative form of the verb, bold type to make important words stand out.

SENTENCE

1 You leave your coat at a pop concert. Use a dictionary to write a simple version of this section of the very official letter which is sent back to you.

We are in receipt of your communication of the 9th.

You are respectfully reminded that the management of this concert hall cannot accept liability for the loss or theft of any item upon the premises.

In the light of this, we beg to inform you that we are unable to proceed with any liability action at this time.

2 You need to fill out a form to apply for a passport. Use a dictionary and write what these official-sounding words and phrases really mean.

visible, distinguishing marks   endorse   place of issue   citizenship   country of residence

3 Write sentences of your own to show what the words really mean.

WORD

1 Add 'ed' to these words. Use a dictionary to check your answers.

walk   jump   climb   store   hop   stop   pat   stir

2 Which words double their final consonants?

3 Add 'er' to these words. Use a dictionary to check your answers.

win   clean   swim   bank   rub   shop   wet   fat

4 Add 'y' to these words. Use a dictionary to check your answers.

chat   gum   skin   dog

5 Decide how many syllables each word contains and write a rule about words which double their final consonant when word building.

Using time in the novel – writing flashbacks

1 Re-read the passage from *The Eagle of the Ninth* (page 50). Write about what happened in the arena the day before as a flashback. Follow the four boxes. Start in present time, go to flashback then return to the present.

Remember:

Collect details of the Roman way of life from the passage.

Marcus is waiting for the slave

He remembers the roar of the crowd in the arena

Describe what happened in the arena on the previous day

Continue the story of Marcus and the slave in the present

Writing about controversial issues

2 Write what you feel about either 'Should children be allowed to work at any age?' or 'Should we pay to give the rest of the world clean water?' Use information collected from page 52 or page 56 to back your arguments. Use the note-making skills learned in this section.

3 Write a newspaper article outlining the dangers of baby-sitting for young people.

◆ Use information collected from page 56 to back your argument.

◆ Have you used words and phrases which will develop your argument, e.g. 'therefore', 'consequently', 'as a result', 'obviously'?

◆ Have you used words and phrases which will move your argument on, e.g. 'but', 'alternatively', 'however', 'nevertheless', 'it could be argued'?

Using different genres for ideas – humour and science fiction

4 Write a piece of science fiction, about an alien emerging from its spacecraft, keeping your reader in suspense. You could use an idea you have seen in a film. Follow the plan of the passage on page 48, e.g.

Paragraph	Description	Reaction
1	Alien slowly comes out.	Author is terrified – cannot move. Cannot really see it.
2	Slowly, more comes out.	People run away in fear.
3	Slowly more of the alien comes out.	Man is more terrified.

5 Continue with the story of *The Phantom Tollbooth* (page 54) in the same style.

Remember:

Humour comes from the events, e.g. funny things that happen; from language, e.g. jokes; and from characters, e.g. the way they dress, how they look and how they behave.

6 Make a film script of *The Phantom Tollbooth* (page 54). Write the stage instructions and design the costumes and sets to make sure the final production is as funny as possible.

Handy hints for planning a story

Type of story
What type of story are you planning to write?
◆ adventure, science fiction, historical, humorous, etc.

Readers?
Who will be your audience?
◆ how will this influence the style you choose?

Setting?
◆ where and when will the story take place?

Characters?
◆ who will they be?
◆ what will they be like?
◆ will they change in the story?

Plot?
◆ what will happen in the story?
◆ how will it begin?
◆ what will happen in the main part of the story?
◆ how will it end?

How are you getting on with the skills in the chart? If you need extra practice try the numbered activities.

Grammar and punctuation	Contracting sentences – summary	1
	Conditionals	2
	Using conditionals	3
	Note-making	4
	Official language – words and expressions	5
Spelling, phonics and vocabulary	Spelling rules – 'ible' and 'able'	6
	Spelling rules – 'i' before 'e'	7
	Mnemonics	8
	Language change over time	9
	Spelling rules – doubling letters	10

1 *a)* Read this passage and write down, as briefly as possible, the four reasons why people do not like living in the city.

People are leaving the city all the time to live in the country. They say that the city is much too noisy and dirty for their children and that there is far too much crime and vandalism. They feel safer in the country. Many people can afford cheaper housing out of the city and the job prospects are better. Many say that they will never return.

b) Think up and write a suitable title for your summary.

2 Copy these sentences and underline the conditional verbs.

Lynn will go to school tomorrow. She asked if her mother would write a note. She would try to talk to her if possible. Her sister went to school yesterday to collect some work. Lynn should be well enough to return to school if the doctor says so.

3 Copy these sentences and underline the conditional verbs.
   a) She would go to the party if her mother let her. She will go to the party. She went to the party.
   b) I should be there by eight o'clock. I will be there by eight o'clock. I was there by eight o'clock.
   c) He would travel by train if he had enough money. He will travel by train. He travelled by train.

Explain how the meanings of these groups of sentences are different because of the different uses of the verbs.

4 *a)* Write out what these notes about school mean.

    geog PE Head lab

  b) Write out in full these notes about days and months.

    Feb Wed Jan

  c) How are the other days of the week and months written in note form?

5 Rewrite these official-sounding sentences in a clearer way, using a dictionary, if necessary.

  a) Further to the receipt of your credit card payment of £100 we have pleasure in forwarding the goods ordered.

  b) We apologise to our customers for any inconvenience suffered.

6 *a)* Add 'ible' or 'able' to the following.

    vis _ _ _ _   poss _ _ _ _   change _ _ _ _
    compat _ _ _ _   accept _ _ _ _   understand _ _ _ _
    adjust _ _ _ _   divis _ _ _ _

  b) Which words take 'ible' or 'able'? Write a rule explaining this and find three more examples of 'ible' and 'able' words.

7 *a)* Copy these words, writing in the 'ei' or 'ie' as appropriate.

    misch _ _ f   c _ _ ling   th _ _ f   rec _ _ ve   s _ _ ze
    fr _ _ nd   gr _ _ f   h _ _ ght   s _ _ ge   p _ _ r
    p _ _ ce   for _ _ gn   n _ _ ther   n _ _ ghbour

  b) Write a rule based on what you have discovered.

8 Invent some mnemonics to help you to spell the words. Use the words in brackets for ideas.

  business (bus) great (eat) young (you) friend (end)
  across between around inside through

9 Look up these words in a dictionary. Explain how their meanings have changed over time.

  ancient horrible ghastly awful mystery

10 *a)* Copy these verbs.

    to: chip run swim stop shop talk stir bore pat hope

  b) Write them in sentences using different verb tenses, e.g. 'Today I..., I will ..., She was... '. Which words double their last letter when word building?

Handy hints for spelling

- ◆ Is the word spelt as it sounds? Does it contain any phonemes you already know?

- ◆ Does the word look right? Do you know any other words like it?

- ◆ Can you break the word into smaller parts? Which is the most difficult part of the word?

- ◆ Do you know what the word means?

- ◆ Have you used a word book or dictionary to help you?

LOOK SAY COVER WRITE CHECK

Cinderilla

This version of Cinderilla, or The Little Glass Slipper, *was first published in 1729 in England.*

There was once upon a time a gentleman who married for the second time. His new wife was the proudest woman that was ever known. She was a widow and had two daughters of her own, almost exactly the same as their mother – proud and vain. Our gentleman had his own daughter, of beautiful sweetness and kindness, which she took from her own mother.

As soon as the wedding was over, the new wife began to show her real character. She could not bear the good qualities of the pretty girl, mainly because they made her own daughters all the more hated by those in the village. So she made the poor girl do the hardest work in the house. She cleaned the dishes and stands, cleaned all the floors, was maid to her sisters and for herself had only the smallest, coldest room in the attic with straw for a bed.

Her sisters slept in fine rooms with marble floors, upon beds of the latest fashions, and they all had full-length looking-glasses so they could admire themselves from head to foot. The poor girl did not complain; she bore all patiently and dared not tell her father, who would have told her off because her step-mother ruled him entirely. When the girl had done her work, she would go quietly to the chimney corner and sit among the cinders. Her nasty step-sisters started to call her Cinderbreech and her nickname became Cinderilla. Whatever they called her, she was still a hundred times prettier than her sisters though they wore the most beautiful clothes.

Now it happened that the King's son gave a ball and invited all the best persons in the land. The young ladies were of course invited, and spent many hours choosing their dresses. This caused Cinderilla much extra work.

Cinderilla advised them the best in the world and dressed them. As she was doing this they said to her, "Cinderilla. Would you not like to go to the ball?"

"Ah," she said. "You only joke with me. It is not for such as I to go to the ball."

"You are right," they all said. "It would make the people laugh to see a Cinderbreech at a ball!"

At last the happy day came; they went to court, and Cinderilla followed them with her eyes as long as she could, and when she had lost sight of them, she fell a-crying.

TEXT

1 How are the characters of the mother and her two daughters the same?

2 *a)* Why did the stepmother not like Cinderilla?
   b) What did she do to show her dislike?

3 *a)* How did Cinderilla behave when her stepmother gave her things to do?
   b) What does this show about the kind of person she was?

4 Explain how Cinderilla got her nickname.

5 *a)* Describe how the sisters treat Cinderilla when they know she cannot go to the ball.
   b) How does Cinderilla reply to them?
   c) How do you know how she really feels?

6 *a)* Write down the words and expressions to show this is a fairytale,
      e.g. Once upon a time.
   b) Compare this version of the story with Roald Dahl's version on page 64.

SENTENCE

1 Copy this passage. Circle the prepositions and underline the connectives.

The plane was on the runway while the pilot waited for the all-clear. He was in the cabin talking to the crew because they needed the new plan. Inside the plane, the passengers knew nothing so continued to eat and drink. Outside, the luggage was being removed but nobody knew why. However, soon it was all clear.

2 Replace the prepositions in the following sentences to change the meaning, e.g. 'under' changed to 'over' makes a big difference, and explain the change.

   a) My mum walked in the room. (out of, through, around)
   b) She looked at a box. (in, on, beside)
   c) The money was inside. (outside, beside, on top)

WORD

1 *a)* Find what these prefixes mean. **tri anti ultra sub retro mono semi**
   b) Write down two examples of words which contain each of these prefixes.

2 *a)* Which suffixes do these words have in common?

   geography geology biology autobiography archaeology

   b) Look in a dictionary to find out what the suffixes mean.
   c) Find other examples of words using these suffixes.

3 *a)* Make words using these root words. **approve appear appoint**
   b) Circle the root words and underline the suffixes and prefixes.
   c) Write sentences using the new words to show you understand what they mean.

Cinderella

This modern Cinderella is not quite the same gentle creature as in the traditional story.

She bellowed "Help!" and "Let me out!"
The Magic Fairy heard her shout.
Appearing in a blaze of light,
She said, "My dear, are you all right?"
"All right?" cried Cindy. "Can't you see
I feel as rotten as can be!"
She beat her fist against the wall,
And shouted, "Get me to the Ball!
There is a Disco at the Palace!
The rest have gone and I am jalous!
I want a dress! I want a coach!
And earrings and a diamond brooch!
And silver slippers, two of those!
And lovely nylon panty-hose!
Done up like that I'll guarantee
The handsome Prince will fall for me!"
The Fairy said, "Hang on a tick,"
She gave her wand a mighty flick
And quickly, in no time at all,
Cindy was at the Palace Ball!
It made the Ugly Sisters wince
To see her dancing with the Prince.
She held him very tight and pressed
herself against his manly chest.
The Prince himself was turned to pulp,
All he could do was gasp and gulp.

Roald Dahl

TEXT

1 *a)* What does Cinderella do to call her fairy godmother?
   b) How can you tell that the fairy has magic powers right from the start?

2 *a)* How does Cinderella reply to her fairy godmother? *b)* What else does she do?
   c) Is it the kind of reaction you expected? Give your reasons.

3 *a)* Explain what Cinderella asks for in this version of the story.
   b) What reason does she give for wanting these things?

4 How do the Ugly Sisters feel about Cinderella at the ball? Which words tell you this?

5 *a)* How does the Prince react to Cinderella? *b)* Which words tell you this?

6 *a)* Give some examples of modern words and phrases which make this version of the story more amusing.
   b) How does the rhyme of the poem help to make you laugh?

7 Describe how the Cinderella in this extract is different from the character in the version on page 62.

SENTENCE

1 Simple sentences can be made into interesting, complex sentences when detail is added, e.g. She was terrified, her eyes were staring and she looked pale.
   Now do the same with this sentence: He was in pain. Make a list of how the person might look, what the person might say, how the person might act.

2 Write a paragraph of interesting sentences describing the following.
   a) Your teacher who realises you have just played a trick on him/her.
   b) A man who has just had his brand-new car damaged.
   c) Your next-door neighbour who has just won the lottery.

WORD

1 Use the parts of words from Box A to add to these roots.
   star aholic agram friendly speak burger athon

   a) How many new words can you make, e.g. superstar? *b)* What do they mean?

Box A:	semi super techno computer euro hyper video

2 Which of these words actually exist? Look in a dictionary and write their meanings.

3 *a)* Invent five more new words of your own to describe school or your computer games.
   b) Make a dictionary of these new words, putting them in alphabetical order and writing a definition.

Computerella

This modern version of Cinderella takes a quirky look at how the Fairy Godmother might behave now.

Narrator: Poor Ella. Her sisters made her work so hard. *(Ella is sweeping the floor and looking sad. Suddenly the Electronic Godmother appears.)*

Ella: Who are you?

Godmother: I'm your Fairy Godmother.

Ella: Fairy Godmother? Oh, I've heard about you. You helped my grandmother, Cinderella.

Godmother: Things have changed since the olden days. Now I'm an Electronic Fairy Godmother *(The Godmother waves her joystick.)*

Ella: I'm very pleased to meet you! Sorry I can't stop working. My sisters get very upset if the work isn't done.

Godmother: Phooey! What about the Prince's message? Couldn't you fix the Royal Computer?

Ella: I might be able to – if I had a chance. But I have to cook and clean and sew and sweep.

Godmother: Don't worry about your cleaning, Ella. My joystick will fast-forward everything and the work will be done in no time. *(The Godmother waves her joystick.)*

Ella: That was fast! Thank you! Now I will go to the Palace.

Godmother: Here are some things you might need. *(She waves her joystick, and some computer disks and a mouse appear.)* I used to turn pumpkins into coaches. These days I have much more fun!

Ella: Thanks again, and goodbye. *(Ella leaves.)*

Hazel Edwards

TEXT

1 What is different about the fairy godmother in this version of Cinderella? How do you know?

2 What tells you straight away that this story of Cinderella will have the same features as the others?

3 What is the problem at the palace? How can Cinderella help?

4 How does the fairy godmother solve Cinderella's problems and get her to the palace?

5 *a)* When the fairy godmother makes magic, what does she make appear?
b) How is this different from what the traditional fairy godmother does?

6 *a)* How is this version different in the way it is written?
b) Which version of the story did you find the funniest and which the most serious? Why?
c) Which version did you like the most? Give your reasons.

SENTENCE

1 Which of these examples are phrases and which are clauses?

a) the bus ticket   *b)* who was holding a bus ticket   *c)* until he scored a goal
d) the roaring crowd   *e)* jumping up and down in excitement

2 Match up the phrases from these two sets. Join them with a verb to write interesting sentences.

Set 1:	my little sister black cats flowers in bloom
Set 2:	in the park outside the house to my dad

3 Write sentences to include these clauses.
a) while he eats his dinner   *b)* until I return from my holiday
c) because it is not modern   *d)* if you sit next to me
e) so that he could work for his father

WORD

1 Copy out this joke and punctuate it correctly.

ive just seen a man with a lemon in his ear

a lemon stuck in his ear what did you do

I went up to him and asked why he had a lemon in his ear

what did he say

he said well youve heard of a man with a hearing aid – well im the man with the lemonade

2 Explain how the joke works. Use the words 'homophone' or 'pun' in your explanation.

Getting Things into Perspective

It is hard to imagine that what we see is different from what other creatures see, but this extract explores this idea.

It isn't only cameras which see things differently from the way we see them. Creatures likely to get eaten have eyes on the sides of their heads, with wide-angle lenses to see all round.

The eyes of animals which hunt them are more to the front, giving them 'binocular' vision (both eyes look at the same thing) and their eyes are shaped like telescopic lenses. Telescopic lenses, or eyes, which see a smaller area from the same viewpoint, make less of the effects of perspective.

Bees can see ultraviolet light. Electric eels see the world through distortions of their magnetic fields (a very real sixth sense!). Man, with the aid of X-rays, can see right through things. Australian aboriginal artists, who had never heard of X-rays, drew animals with their backbones and internal organs showing. Other artists, who also want to draw things how they are, rather than just how they look, draw people the same size … however far away they may be. Some artists have drawn people they regard as the most important, the biggest. Others try to draw things how they feel rather than how they look.

A little girl who had been running barefoot in wet grass drew herself with huge spread toes and her legs pressed against her skirt.

Colin Caket

TEXT

1 *a)* Where are the eyes of animals which are likely to get hunted?

   b) Why are they in this position?

2 *a)* What do you think binocular vision means?

   b) Why do animals who hunt have this kind of vision?

3 Give three examples from the passage of different ways people or animals see things.

4 What kinds of artists draw things as they are rather than they look? Give an example.

5 What example does the author give to show that some people draw things how they feel rather than how they look?

6 Find examples of these features of an explanatory text in the passage: uses diagrams, uses technical language, gives examples.

SENTENCE

1 Copy out this passage and punctuate it correctly.

   tracy my sister was emptying her school bag when she got home on tuesday

   where did you get this pound coin from my mother asked its more than your pocket money

   oh that fred gave it to me I was doing him a favour replied tracy stroking the cats neck

   what exactly were you doing for him mum said

   I was twisting his arm and he asked me to stop tracy said smiling

WORD

1 Write out these words inserting 'ough'. Check your spellings in a dictionary.

   pl _ _ _ _   th _ _ _ _ t   c _ _ _ _   br _ _ _ _ t   r _ _ _ _   b _ _ _ _   f _ _ _ _ t

2 Sort the words into three groups according to the different sounds the letter string 'ough' makes, e.g. does 'rough' sound the same as 'bough'?

3 Write out these words, deciding if you need a single or a double 'r'.

   ma ___ y   Ha ___ y   eve ___ y   a ___ ive   ca ___ ot   te ___ or   bu ___ y

   mi ___ or   so ___ y   tomo ___ ow   ve ___ y   hu ___ y   cu ___ ant

   Check your spellings in a dictionary.

4 Find the answers to these crossword clues.

   A noise made by ducks.   The wife of a king.   A place where fish are kept.
   A padded covering for a bed.   What you need to get an answer.

5 Which two letters are found together in every word?

Rules for Using the Internet

Surfing the Internet is an increasingly popular pastime, but one where rules still need to apply.

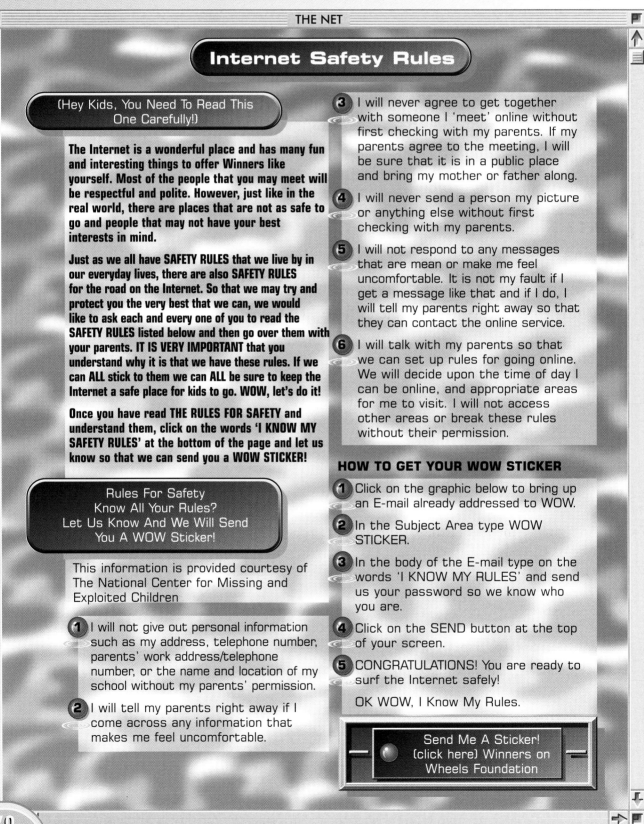

THE NET

Internet Safety Rules

(Hey Kids, You Need To Read This One Carefully!)

The Internet is a wonderful place and has many fun and interesting things to offer Winners like yourself. Most of the people that you may meet will be respectful and polite. However, just like in the real world, there are places that are not as safe to go and people that may not have your best interests in mind.

Just as we all have SAFETY RULES that we live by in our everyday lives, there are also SAFETY RULES for the road on the Internet. So that we may try and protect you the very best that we can, we would like to ask each and every one of you to read the SAFETY RULES listed below and then go over them with your parents. IT IS VERY IMPORTANT that you understand why it is that we have these rules. If we can ALL stick to them we can ALL be sure to keep the Internet a safe place for kids to go. WOW, let's do it!

Once you have read THE RULES FOR SAFETY and understand them, click on the words 'I KNOW MY SAFETY RULES' at the bottom of the page and let us know so that we can send you a WOW STICKER!

Rules For Safety
Know All Your Rules?
Let Us Know And We Will Send
You A WOW Sticker!

This information is provided courtesy of The National Center for Missing and Exploited Children

1 I will not give out personal information such as my address, telephone number, parents' work address/telephone number, or the name and location of my school without my parents' permission.

2 I will tell my parents right away if I come across any information that makes me feel uncomfortable.

3 I will never agree to get together with someone I 'meet' online without first checking with my parents. If my parents agree to the meeting, I will be sure that it is in a public place and bring my mother or father along.

4 I will never send a person my picture or anything else without first checking with my parents.

5 I will not respond to any messages that are mean or make me feel uncomfortable. It is not my fault if I get a message like that and if I do, I will tell my parents right away so that they can contact the online service.

6 I will talk with my parents so that we can set up rules for going online. We will decide upon the time of day I can be online, and appropriate areas for me to visit. I will not access other areas or break these rules without their permission.

HOW TO GET YOUR WOW STICKER

1 Click on the graphic below to bring up an E-mail already addressed to WOW.

2 In the Subject Area type WOW STICKER.

3 In the body of the E-mail type on the words 'I KNOW MY RULES' and send us your password so we know who you are.

4 Click on the SEND button at the top of your screen.

5 CONGRATULATIONS! You are ready to surf the Internet safely!

OK WOW, I Know My Rules.

Send Me A Sticker!
(click here) Winners on
Wheels Foundation

TEXT

1 Why do you think it says that it is important for children to read the rules carefully?

2 *a)* What is the reward for having read the safety rules?

b) How do you know that this extract is meant to be shown on a computer screen?

3 From where has the information used to write the rules been taken?

4 Why do you think so many words are written in capital letters?

5 Explain why you think the advice each rule gives is important.

6 *a)* Explain how you would get a 'WOW' sticker.

b) How are these instructions different from the rest of the extract?

7 What clues can you find in the passage that tell you that this website was designed for young people in wheelchairs?

SENTENCE

1 Each of these words can mean two things. Write two sentences to show this.

seal   trunk   ring   fine   ruler   pound

2 Write sentences to show how these words have changed their meanings.

pretty   naughty   villain

3 Write sentences to show the different meanings of these words.

bad   cool   wicked   gross   trainer

4 These words have changed their meaning over the past twenty years. Write sentences to show the old and new meanings of these words.

pop   charts   jockey   rock   band   album

WORD

1 Add 'full' to the end of these nouns to make them adjectives. Check your answers in a dictionary.

hope   joy   dread   fright   help

2 Write what happens to the spelling of 'full' when you add it as a suffix.

3 *a)* Now take the adjectives you have made and make them into adverbs by adding 'ly'.

b) Does anything happen to the spelling of the root word or the suffix you have added?

4 Write a set of rules which would help someone who was finding spelling words with a single or a double 'l' difficult.

Writing rules and instructions

1 Follow these instructions to make a paper aeroplane. Now write a set of instructions for somebody else. You will probably find it helpful to describe each stage step-by-step and to number your instructions.

Remember:

List what you need first. Make sure you number the steps and follow a logical sequence. Use bullet points to make things clearer. Use imperative verbs and clear, short sentences.

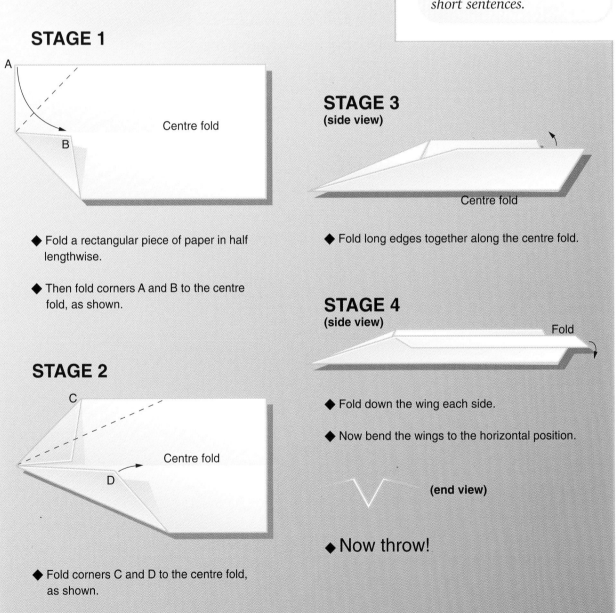

STAGE 1

Centre fold

◆ Fold a rectangular piece of paper in half lengthwise.

◆ Then fold corners A and B to the centre fold, as shown.

STAGE 2

Centre fold

◆ Fold corners C and D to the centre fold, as shown.

STAGE 3
(side view)

Centre fold

◆ Fold long edges together along the centre fold.

STAGE 4
(side view)

Fold

◆ Fold down the wing each side.

◆ Now bend the wings to the horizontal position.

(end view)

◆ Now throw!

Comparison of a treatment of a theme

2 Choose a fairytale (other than *Cinderella*). Write three different versions of the story. These versions might be:

◆ A traditional version using fairytale language.
◆ A poem.
◆ An article in a magazine about what happened.
◆ A humorous version.
◆ A modern-day version.
◆ A playscript.
◆ A version in which the roles are swopped around, e.g. the villain becomes the hero.

Writing reviews for real audiences

3 Imagine that a group in your class decides to start a Book Club.

a) Design a badge for the club and write a set of rules.
b) Design a reading certificate which can be awarded when a member has read ten books.
c) Write reviews of your favourite books to encourage others to read them, e.g. Three Great Books – Not To Be Missed!

Reviews could include:

◆ Certificates to be awarded to the author with reasons for the prize.
◆ Letters to the author telling him or her what you thought was good and what could be better.
◆ Problem pages from characters in the books, discussing the problems they had.
◆ Posters advertising the good points of the books and recommending them.
◆ Blurbs for the back covers of your favourite books (see Handy hints).

Handy hints for writing a blurb

Have you collected 'blurbs' and analysed them? Have you found features such as:

◆ direct quotations from the book?
◆ quotations from a reviewer?
◆ quotations from the opening to interest you?
◆ questions to interest you in the story?
◆ information about the author?
◆ information about awards it may have won?
◆ other books in the series?

◆ Is it clear who the audience is for your blurb?

◆ Does your blurb really tell the reader what he or she wants to know?

◆ Does your blurb give too much of the story away?

◆ Does your blurb really make you want to read the book? If so, why?

How are you getting on with the skills in the chart? If you need extra practice try the numbered activities.

Grammar and punctuation	Prepositions and connectives	1
	Simple to complex sentences	2
	Revision of phrases and clauses	3
	How words change meaning	4
	Revision of punctuation	5
Spelling, phonics and vocabulary	Roots, prefixes and suffixes	6
	Wordplay – jokes and puns	7
	Building words – letter strings	8
	Single or double 'l'	9

1 *a)* Copy this passage. Circle the prepositions and underline the connectives.

My cat sat on the wall outside. She was watching the birds and their chicks under the bushes, although she also noticed the children in the garden next door. It looked as if she would go hungry until my mum arrived with the shopping.

b) Use different connectives and prepositions for two sentences. Explain how the meaning changes.

2 Write three simple sentences describing how people might feel if they were lost or had won the lottery. List more detail about the scenes and write much longer, more interesting sentences.

3 *a)* Match up the phrases in Set 1 to those in Set 2 and join them with a verb to make interesting sentences:

b) Add clauses to these sentences to make them more interesting.

At 18 you can vote.   Do not watch that film.
The rainforest is slowly being destroyed.

Set 1:   into pieces
from the cave   small flames

Set 2:   strange noises
in the darkness   my favourite toy

4 Write sentences to show what you understand by these words. Then find out what they originally meant.

location   shot   exposure   still   screen

5 Copy out and punctuate this passage correctly.

three children were digging deep into the sand on the beach

youre working very hard children i said to them whats the hurry

one girl stopped and replied weve got to the hole caved in

cant your dad help you I wondered

well ask him when weve dug him out the girls brother replied

6 Find the meaning of these prefixes and suffixes.

tele   circu   dis   post   mis   mal
able   ful   scope   graph

Write down two examples of words which contain each prefix and suffix.

7 Copy out and punctuate these jokes, setting them out correctly.

a) How many can get this bird Toucan.
b) Where is Felixtowe on the end of Felix foot

8 *a)* Add the letter string 'gu' to these words.

va _ _ e   ton _ _ e   dis _ _ ise   pla _ _ e   epilo _ _ e

Find out what the words mean and write them in sentences.

b) Add 'gu' to the beginning of these words.

_ _ ess   _ _ ard   _ _ itar   _ _ arantee   _ _ ardian
_ _ ide   _ _ erilla

Find out what the words mean and write them in sentences.

9 *a)* Add 'full' to the end of these words.

grate _ _ _ _   shame _ _ _ _   pain _ _ _ _   awe _ _ _ _

b) What happens to the spelling of the suffix?
c) What happens when you add 'ly' to the new words in a)? Check your answers in a dictionary.

Handy hints for spelling

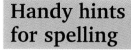

◆ Is the word spelt as it sounds? Does it contain any phonemes you already know?

◆ Does the word look right? Do you know any other words like it?

◆ Can you break the word into smaller parts? Which is the most difficult part of the word?

◆ Do you know what the word means?

◆ Have you used a word book or dictionary to help you?

LOOK   SAY   COVER   WRITE   CHECK

The Machine Gunners

This story is set during the Second World War. Chas and his friends collect items to do with the war. The police and the Home Guard try to stop them.

"Please, sir, Mum says come quick. There's a deep hole in our garden and there's a ticking coming from it."

Fatty looked distinctly worried. Airplane engines was airplane engines and needed protecting from thieving kids, but unexploded bombs was unexploded bombs.

"Hurry, sir! There's little kids all round it, looking down the hole."

Fatty grabbed his shoulders and shook him roughly.

"Where, where? Take me, take me!"

"Please, sir, no, sir. Mum says I mustn't go back there, in case it goes off. I've got to go to me gran's, sir, but the bomb's at 19, Marston Road."

Fatty went off at a wobbling run, his gasmask case flogging his broad bottom. Before he was out of sight, Chas was at the engine. Its realness was overwhelming. There were German words on the cowling. Öl was the only one he could recognise. Everything was bigger close to. The twisted prop-blades curled into the air like palm-leaves. The red spinner, which he had thought as carryable as a rugby-ball, now seemed as big as a brewery-barrel. He tugged at it; it came off so far and then stuck. He heaved again at the shiny red newness. It still resisted.

"Nazi pigs!" he screamed, as his hand slipped and the blood came. He picked up a lump of brickwork, four bricks still cemented together, and, raising it above his head, flung it at the spinner. The beautiful red thing crushed in, but it still wouldn't budge. He hit it again. Another great white flaking dent appeared. It was a mess now, hardly worth having. But still it refused to come off.

There was a sudden roar of rage from behind. Fatty Hardy had returned, sweaty face working. Chas ran.

He wasn't greatly worried. Hardy was puffing already; he wouldn't last fifty yards. The only worry was the piles of rubble underfoot. If he fell, Hardy would have him. Placing his feet carefully, he ran towards the Wood.

The Wood was in the grounds of West Chirton Hall. At one time, his father said, the people at the Hall had owned everything. But then the factories came, and the council estate, and the owners of the Hall just curled up and died for shame. Now the house itself was just a hole in the ground lined with brick, and a black cinder floor. There was a big water-tank full of rusty water, and nothing else.

Robert Westall

TEXT

1 What does Chas make Fatty think is down the hole?

2 *a)* Why does Chas tell lies to the policeman? *b)* What did he want the policeman to do? *c)* What did he want to do himself?

3 *a)* How was the policeman feeling when he came back? How do you know? *b)* How did Chas react to this?

4 Where did Chas run to? Why was Chas not worried that the policeman would follow him?

5 Copy three pieces of evidence from the passage to show that this story is set in the time of the Second World War.

6 Write about which parts of the passage are serious, funny and descriptive.

SENTENCE

1 Change these instructions from the passive to the active tense.

One egg was taken by the chef and it was mixed with mustard and a pinch of white sugar. Some vinegar was then measured into a large bowl and was slowly added to the rest of the ingredients. Finally some salt, olive oil and pepper were whisked in.

2 Change these instructions from the active to the passive tense.

Empty the contents into a large mixing bowl. Add 190 ml of hot water. Mix thoroughly to make a dough. Place on a lightly floured surface. Knead and stretch the dough until completely smooth (approximately 5 minutes).

3 *a)* What differences do you notice between the two versions? *b)* Which is the better tense for instructions?

WORD

1 *a)* Write out the alphabet.   *b)* Circle the vowels. What sounds do these letters make? *c)* Write some words using long vowel sounds, e.g. 'acorn'.

2 *a)* Write these words and circle the first vowel.   **apple egg in on orange** *b)* What sound do these letters make? How are the short vowel sounds different from the long sounds?

3 *a)* Add 'le' to these short vowel sounds.   **bat gab set net rip rid mid top** *b)* Check your spelling in a dictionary. What do you notice happens?

4 *a)* Add 'le' to these long vowel sounds.   **gab stab bib trif bug rif** Check your spelling in a dictionary. What do you notice happens?

b) Write a rule to explain the differences in spelling when adding 'le' to short or long vowel sounds.

The Stones of Muncaster Cathedral

This writer is a stone-mason restoring an old cathedral, waiting for the helicopter to bring the weather-vane for the top of the spire. But things don't quite go to plan.

The cathedral green was full now; you couldn't see the grass any more; it was covered with humans, crawling wi' them, like a chucked-out chicken leg crawls wi' flies.

"I hope they get what they've come for," said Billy bitterly, and I found my stomach tightening. Then he cocked an ear and said, "Here it comes."

There was the slight faint blatting of a helicopter, and we heard a satisfied murmur rise from the crowd, like a sigh, so far below it was.

The blatting grew louder, echoing around Cathedral Close's tall buildings, so there seemed half a dozen helicopters not one.

"Check my sling, Joe," said Billy nervously. I checked his safety-sling, the other end fastened to the scaffolding, and then he checked mine.

The helicopter was coming in about a hundred feet above us, the gilded weather-vane dangling beneath it like a great obscene fish-hook, and the RAF bloke looking out of the big hatch in the side, judging the distance, telling the pilot what to do through his throat microphone. I took a look at the pilot; he looked a steady intent chap; I liked the careful way he watched what he was doing.

Then the chopper was right overhead, and Billy's mouth was opening and shutting and I couldn't hear a word he was saying, for the noise of the chopper's engine and blades. Every blat of it hit your ears like a fist, making you want to cower. I began to wish we'd used ear-plugs, but it was too late now. And the pressure from the rotor blades coming downwards, pushing you flat so you had to struggle to keep your balance. Never again, I told myself; then the weather-vane was on its way down to us, swinging like a pendulum, not far or fast, but I remembered the weight of it.

Billy and I were just reaching up to steady it, and guide it into the socket on top of the steeple we'd got ready for it…

When it happened.

The weather-vane swung out away from us, dipped a few feet, swung back far too low, and caught under the scaffolding with a terrible clang. The scaffolding was hooked like a fish. And in a flash, the rising air had pushed the helicopter upwards again.

The whole scaffold heaved up under us like the deck of a ship when a wave hits it. There was a terrible grating as it tried to break free of the steeple. We were thrown on our faces; without the safety-slings, we'd have gone clean over the edge of the planking.

Robert Westall

TEXT

1 *a)* Why was the cathedral green crowded?

   b) What were the people so curious about?

2 How can you tell in the first paragraph that the writer is speaking in his normal voice?

3 Find evidence in the passage to indicate that the men were builders.

4 *a)* How can you tell that the helicopter made a very loud noise?

   b) What else made it hard for the men to keep their balance?

5 *a)* Explain how the helicopter caused the disaster.   *b)* How did the men survive?

6 Write about how this passage is different from the passage by Robert Westall on page 76. Think about whether it is written in the first or third person, the time in which it is set, whether it is funny or serious all the time, the kind of language used by the writer and the subject of the story.

SENTENCE

1 *a)* From which countries do these words originally come?

   kiosk   coffee   tea   bamboo   budgerigar   trek   veranda   yacht

   b) Write what they mean and use the words in sentences.

2 Find out the derivation of the days of the week. Your dictionary will help.
   Here is one: Thursday was originally the day of Thor.

3 Match up these words to their correct derivation. Find out what the ancient words originally meant.

Word:	Derivation:
expect just finished	bios (Greek) sensus (Latin) klima (Greek)
climate sensitive biography	expectare (Latin) justus (Latin) finis (Latin)

WORD

1 Complete these words using 'tion'.

   na _ _ _ _   sta _ _ _ _   opera _ _ _ _   invita _ _ _ _   educa _ _ _ _

2 *a)* Which of the words above come from a verb, e.g. 'to operate'?

   b) What changes take place when the verb is changed to a noun with the ending 'tion'?

3 Copy these words, adding 'sion'.

   televi _ _ _ _   revi _ _ _ _   confu _ _ _ _   divi _ _ _ _   deci _ _ _ _

4 *a)* Copy these words, writing in 'ial'.

   essent _ _ _   spec _ _ _   part _ _ _   torrent _ _ _   offic _ _ _

   b) Which letters come before 'ial' to make the 'sh' sound?

Naming a Chinese Cat

This story has been translated from a Chinese fable.

Long ago in the mountains of China there lived an old man and his large family. The master of the Chi-Yen family was very fond of his large, striped ginger cat. He called it Tiger.

One day, he was outside his house, soaking up the sunshine, stroking Tiger. The cat purred contentedly on his knee. A visitor, a stranger to the village, passed by and stopped to stroke the cat. He asked its name.

'But a tiger is a wild, ferocious beast. A dragon is more mysterious. Your cat is more like a dragon. Why not change its name?' The host thanked the man and continued to stroke his cat.

Some days later, another stranger to the village saw the cat and, having heard the argument about the cat's name and character, said: 'A dragon is more mysterious than a tiger. It flies high into the sky and rests on the clouds. The clouds are therefore greater than the dragon. Why not call your cat Cloud?' The host smiled, thanked the man and watched as the cat played in the sun.

All week, people in the village dropped by, constantly changing the cat's name. One idea followed another:
'The wind blows the clouds about. Wind is the greater thing. Call your cat Wind.'
'But a wall can hold back a wind. The best name for your cat is Wall.'
'Yes, walls are strong, but they can crumble. Cats chase and kill rats. Rat is the best name for your cat, Master Chi-Yen.'

At last the old man laughed. 'Stop! Stop! Look at the animal, my friends. A cat is a cat. It lives to kill the rats in the village. It is my friend but it is also a wild beast. Listen to it howling in the night as if it were still in the jungle. Why try to change what it really is?'

TEXT

1 Why do you think the old man had given the cat its original name?

2 What reasons did the first two strangers give for wanting to change the cat's name?

3 Explain the final three people's suggestions for names and why they thought they were suitable.

4 *a)* How did the old man react to their suggestions at first? *b)* How did he finally react?

5 A fable tries to teach us something by telling us a story.
Explain what this story about a cat is trying to teach us.

6 This passage and *Macavity the Mystery Cat* are both texts about cats.
Explain how they are both very different by commenting on what the authors are trying to do in their writing and the way in which the two texts are written.

SENTENCE

1 Add a sentence before these clauses.

    a) … unless you buy me a cake.   *b)* … if I ever see you again.

    c) … while they were sitting on the beach.   *d)* … whether she liked it or not.

2 Now turn the sentences around, writing the clause at the beginning,
e.g. 'Unless you buy me a cake…' .

3 If two sentences are about the same person they can often be joined by 'who',
e.g. 'He is a friendly boy. He likes dogs' could become 'He is a friendly boy who likes dogs'. Do this with these sentences.

    a) Bob has a new girlfriend. She is a racing driver.

    b) Fred went to the Headteacher. She sent him home.

    c) The manager ran to the goalkeeper. He was rolling about in agony.

WORD

1 What is the job of the following people who: **act teach sing invent collect**?
Check in a dictionary to make sure you are using the correct ending.

2 *a)* Copy these words. Use a dictionary to check. Decide whether to use 'er' or 'or' at the end of the word. **charact _ _ carpent _ _ emper _ _ horr _ _ comput _ _**

    b) Find five more examples of words ending in 'er' or 'or'.

3 *a)* Copy these words. Decide whether to add 'er', 'or', 'our'. Use a dictionary to check your answers. **fav ____ hon ____ hum ____ vap ____ col ____**

    b) Add 'ous' to these words. What happens to the spelling? Use a dictionary to check.

    c) How do Americans spell these particular words?

Macavity the Mystery Cat

Macavity is an elusive cat, so is he really responsible for all the crime in the area?

Macavity's a Mystery Cat: he's called the Hidden Paw –
For he's the master criminal who can defy the Law.
He's the bafflement of Scotland Yard, the Flying Squad's despair:
For when they reach the scene of crime - *Macavity's not there!*
Macavity, Macavity, there's no one like Macavity,
He's broken every human law, he breaks the law of gravity.
His powers of levitation would make a fakir stare,
And when you reach the scene of crime – *Macavity's not there!*
But I tell you once and once again, *Macavity's not there!*

Macavity's a ginger cat, he's very tall and thin;
You would know him if you saw him, for his eyes are sunken in.
His brow is deeply lined with thought, his head is highly domed;
His coat is dusty from neglect, his whiskers are uncombed.
He sways his head from side to side, with movements like a snake;
And when you think he's half asleep, he's always wide awake.

Macavity, Macavity, there's no one like Macavity,
For he's a fiend in feline shape, a monster of depravity.
You may meet him in a by-street, you may see him in the square –
But when a crime's discovered, the *Macavity's not there!*

He's outwardly respectable. (They say he cheats at cards.)
And his footprints are not found in any file of Scotland Yard's.
And when the larder's looted, or the jewel-case is rifled,
Or when the milk is missing, or another Peke's been stifled,
Or the greenhouse glass is broken, and the trellis past repair –
Ay, there's the wonder of the thing! Macavity's not there!

T. S. Eliot

TEXT

1 Explain briefly why Macavity is a 'mystery' cat.

2 Use a dictionary to write the meanings of the following words.

levitation   gravity   fakir

3 Imagine you are writing a police report. Describe Macavity.

4 What do you think the poet means when he describes the cat as 'outwardly respectable?' Give an example.

5 Write an account of why someone should find this poem amusing. Look at the details in the poem, the story of the poem, the way that the poem is rhymed.

6 Compare this poem with the story of the Chinese Cat on page 80. Say how they are similar and different. Which one would you recommend to a friend? Why?

SENTENCE

1 Copy out these passages and correctly punctuate them.

a) hello hello hello said the policeman what have we here
   thats a stupid question said the workman its a large hole

b) my teacher was telling us about fractions the other day
   you all know that a half is bigger than a quarter the teacher told us
   no miss I said
   well ill ask you a simple question would you rather have a half of a bar of
   chocolate or a quarter she continued
   id rather have a quarter miss was my answer
   but thats silly explain to me why
   because I dont like chocolate miss I said

WORD

1 Copy these sentences, writing in a good simile.

a) When the bell rang, the class ran out like…   *b)* The noise in the class was like…
c) The cat was as proud as… of its new kittens.   *d)* The tyre was as flat as…

2 Pick out and write the metaphors in this passage. Explain why they are metaphors and not similes.

The girl danced like a feather in the wind. Her eyes were diamonds and her teeth pearls. Everyone said that she was as pretty as a picture. She and the other dancers sailed across the stage and cruised through the performance. They were greeted by a wave of applause at the end. Afterwards, they were dumb … they could say nothing.

The BT Tower

The Telecom Tower is a London landmark, about which there are many interesting facts.

The short and the tall of it

Did you know that every tall building contracts in cold weather and expands in warm weather?

The Tower is no exception to this rule. In the winter, it can be as much as 23 centimetres shorter than it is in the summer.

Designed to sway in the wind

Another characteristic of tall buildings is that they sway from side to side in the wind.

The Tower is designed to sway much less than most high-rise structures – up to 20 centimetres from the vertical, to be precise – so as not to affect the accuracy of the microwave radio transmissions.

An uplifting experience

The two tower lifts in the Tower are among the fastest in Europe. They travel at an incredible 6 metres a second and take just over 30 seconds to whizz you to the top.

During the first year the Tower was open to the public – from 19 May 1966, to 19 May 1967 – they travelled 70,000 kilometres between them, carrying nearly 1 million visitors; 105,000 of whom dined in the revolving restaurant 158 metres above London.

The fare for everyone, whether you were eating or not, was 4 shillings (20p) and half price for children.

Food for thought

A special edition of *The Evening News* during the week the revolving restaurant opened made no mention of the quality of the food, but reported:

'Drinks are about double street level prices and the cheapest meal, the businessman's lunch (with menu in French), costs 30 shillings plus 2s 6d for coffee. Dinner costs around £5 a head.'

See London in 22 minutes

The Presentation Suite (located where the restaurant used to be) is the widest part of the Tower – with a total diameter of almost 20 metres. And yes, it still revolves!

The revolving part is just over 3 metres wide, runs on nylon tyred wheels on circular rails, completes a full circle every 22 minutes and weighs 30 tonnes.

The precision of the rotating mechanism is such that there is a clearance of less than one third of a centimetre between the moving and stationary sections.

In 22 minutes you can see all the major landmarks in London without moving an inch.

- **Tower Bridge**
- **Houses of Parliament**
- **Buckingham Palace**
- **Canary Wharf**
- **The City**
- **St Paul's Cathedral**

The BT Tower

TEXT

1 *a)* Use a dictionary to write the meaning of 'contracts'.

   b) How much does the BT Tower contract? In which season does this happen?

2 Why is it important that the BT Tower should not sway as much as other tall buildings?

3 *a)* How long does it take to travel to the top of the BT Tower in the lift?

   b) Using the figures given to you, work out roughly how tall the building is.

4 How long does it take the room at the top of the Tower to rotate in a full circle?

5 What did this room used to be when the Tower was opened? What is the room called now?

6 Explain how the room at the top of the Tower can rotate. From what are the moving parts made?

SENTENCE

1 Scientific or technical words are often used in advertising, e.g. 'Toothpaste which contains Strontium Acetate and fluoride'.

   a) Write about three advertisements which use this technique. Write the scientific words they use.   *b)* Find out what they mean.

2 Advertising also uses superlatives, e.g. 'the biggest...', 'the most popular...' .

   Find three advertisements that use superlatives and list them.

3 Rewrite the boring bicycle advertisement below. Use more interesting words and phrases to advertise the product on television, e.g. 'Want the latest in...', 'Feeling left out as your friend speeds about? Then get...'

   FOR SALE: mountain bike, big wheels, straight handlebars, good saddle, new brakes, excellent condition. £100 o.n.o.

WORD

1 Change one letter at a time to move from one word to another, e.g. from 'hat' to 'cap' in two moves: 'hat, cat, cap'. Move from 'boy' to 'man' in three moves. Move 'six' to 'ten' in three moves. Move 'milk' to 'wine' in three moves. Move 'mother' to 'father' in three moves. Move 'sun' to 'hot' in four moves.

2 How many words can you find in these words, e.g. carrot contains car and rot (2 words)?

   chocolate (4 possible)   television (4 possible)   grandfather (7 possible)

Using fiction as a model

1 Continue the story of *The Machine Gunners* (page 76), considering the following:

◆ What happens to Chas in the wood?

◆ What does he find? Look at the clues about his interests.

◆ How does he tell his friends?

◆ How does an adventure develop?

2 *The Stones of Muncaster Cathedral* (page 78) is a story of the supernatural. Continue with the story. You could use the flashback technique to go back in time to explain things, or write the diary of the man in the story explaining what and why things happened:

◆ What happens to the helicopter?

◆ What supernatural forces have caused it? Why?

◆ How does the character in the story deal with it and win in the end?

◆ Think about the setting of the old cathedral, what it is like inside when he is making the repairs.

◆ What is the mystery in the past?

Writing to promote something

3 Design and write your own advertisement for television. Decide on your product and think about advertisements which you know and the tricks they use. You can use them, too.

Remember:

◆ *Many advertisements show happy families and often include animals and babies.*

◆ *They use popular people who are successful in their jobs.*

◆ *They often like to focus on luxury and like to make people feel they are different and are setting the trend.*

◆ *Adverts often use scientific and technical words to make the product special and like to say everything is NEW.*

◆ *They use superlatives like 'the greatest', 'the most beautiful'.*

◆ *They might use jokes, or will include a memorable rhyme or phrase.*

Writing about different works by the same author

4 Reread the two passages by Robert Westall.
Make a chart using the headings in the Handy hints.

	'The Machine Gunners'	**'The Stones of Muncaster Cathedral'**
Place	Newcastle area	Unknown
Time	Second World War – Nazis, etc	Modern day – helicopters, etc
Language		

Then use your notes to write about the differences between the two works by this author. Say which piece you like best, giving your reasons.

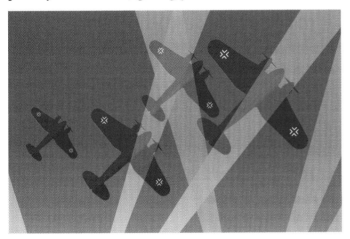

Handy hints for comparing works by the same author

Place
◆ Where are the two texts set?

Time
◆ In which era is each book set?

Language
◆ Is the language simple, poetic, difficult?

Kind of story
◆ Is it historical, modern, fantasy, supernatural, humorous?

Tone
◆ Serious or funny?

Characters
◆ Heroes or villains? Do you like them? Why?

Narrator
◆ First or third person?

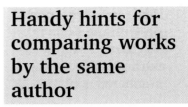

How are you getting on with the skills in the chart? If you need extra practice try the numbered activities.

Grammar and punctuation	Active and passive verbs	1
	Clauses for effects	2
	Language convention – advertising and promotion	3
	Revision of punctuation	4
Spelling, phonics and vocabulary	Short and long vowels	5
	Words containing 'tion', 'ial'	6
	Words containing 'er', 'or', 'our'	7
	Metaphors	8
	Word games	9

1 Rewrite this part of a recipe in the active tense.

The bread dough was shaped by the chef and placed into a lightly greased bread tin. It was then covered by a damp cloth and was left in a warm place for 40 minutes until it was seen to double in size. Whilst the bread was rising, the oven was heated to a temperature of 230°C. Finally the bread was baked for 35 minutes until it sounded hollow when it was tapped.

2 Join these pairs of sentences with 'which', e.g. 'The pen fell on the paper. It got covered with ink.' could become 'The pen fell on the paper which got covered with ink.'

a) I've got a cut on my thumb. It is hurting all the time.

b) My dad's got a horse. It always loses races.

c) The tree blew over in the hurricane. It had been raging all night.

3 *a)* Write down the comparative and superlative forms of these adjectives.

strong   lucky   thin   good   beautiful   lovely   handsome   pleasant

b) Use a dictionary and thesaurus to find as many synonyms as possible that an advertiser might want to use for 'good' and 'big'.

4 Copy out and punctuate this passage correctly.

I saw a gangster film yesterday it was funny marcus said they were all standing there and the gangster was dead

that doesnt sound very funny to me I replied

well they were all saying things about how good he was at robbing people shooting other gangsters and breaking the law

yes well I still dont see what was funny

his best friend stopped them and asked why they hadnt said such nice things about him when he was alive

5 *a)* Write the five vowels on the top of your page and list these words under the correct letter.

mat   hop   pet   cod   kit   rip   not   fat   gap   rob
pip   rod   them   fin   hat   win   us   mad   bit   rat

b) Do these words make long or short sounds?

c) Now add an 'e' to all of these words and write them again under the five vowels. What kind of vowel sound do these words make now?

6 *a)* Copy these words, adding 'tion'.

inven _ _ _ _   **elec** _ _ _ _   **frac** _ _ _ _   **ac** _ _ _ _
ques _ _ _ _   **por** _ _ _ _   **junc** _ _ _ _   **attrac** _ _ _ _

b) Copy these words, adding 'ial'.

soc _ _ _   **essent** _ _ _   **part** _ _ _   **spec** _ _ _

Which letters come before 'ial' to make the 'sh' sound?

7 *a)* What do we call a person who:

instructs   bakes   educates   suffers   commands

b) Write out the correct English spellings of these words, using a dictionary to check.

favor   honer   humor   armor   valor   vaper   color

c) Add 'ous' to these words. What happens to the spelling?

8 Explain these metaphors. What do the authors really mean?

a) The stars are pinpricks in the dark sky.
b) Education is your passport to a good job.
c) The sports car flew into the distance.

9 *a)* How many smaller words can you find in these words?

coffee   pineapple   thermometer

b) Unjumble these animal anagrams.

drib   igert   tikten   pypup

Handy hints for spelling

◆ Is the word spelt as it sounds? Does it contain any phonemes you already know?

◆ Does the word look right? Do you know any other words like it?

◆ Can you break the word into smaller parts? Which is the most difficult part of the word?

◆ Do you know what the word means?

◆ Have you used a word book or dictionary to help you?

LOOK
SAY
COVER
WRITE
CHECK

Glossary

active (form of the verb)

A verb is active when the subject of the verb is actually performing the action in the sentence:

Fred **drove** the car.

Fred is the subject of the sentence. He is the one performing the action. He is driving the car. (See passive)

adjective

An adjective is a describing word. It describes (adds meaning to) a noun:

the **big, red** car.

adjectives   noun

adverb

An adverb is a word or phrase which describes a verb:

He runs.
He runs **quickly**. He runs **slowly**.

adverb

Many adverbs end in 'ly', but not all:

He runs **fast**.

anagram

An anagram is a puzzle in which the letters of a word have been jumbled up:

Granmaa is an anagram of the word **anagram!**

brackets

These punctuation marks ( ) can be used like dashes. They can separate off a part of a sentence or put in an extra example:

He was awarded a prize in school (not before time).

brackets

clause

A clause is a group of words. It can be used as a whole sentence or a part of a sentence. It does not necessarily make a sentence in its own right. It must contain a verb and it has a subject:

Tracey walked home.

subject   verb   object

(See also phrase and notice the difference)

colon

A colon is often used to introduce a list, before someone speaks or instead of a full stop:

He was very cold: the temperature was below zero.

The larder contained: eggs, butter, bread and apples.

Louise said: "What are you doing here?"

comparative

When we compare adjectives, we call them comparative adjectives. For example:

big and **bigger**

One stage further is called the superlative:

biggest

When the adjectives are longer words, these rules do not apply. Instead we use 'more' as in:

more beautiful,

and 'most' as in:

the **most beautiful**.

Words such as 'good' have their own forms:

better, best (See superlative)

conditional (form of the verb)

A conditional verb tells you that the action might happen, because it depends on something or somebody else. 'Should', 'would' and 'could' are the three words which tell you if a verb is conditional.

We **would** go to the cinema if...

I **should** be grateful if you could...

He **could** do his homework although...

conjunction

Conjunctions are joining words in sentences. They link short sentences together. The commonest conjunctions are 'and' and 'but':

She wanted to go for a swim **but** it was too cold.

conjunction

connective

These are words and phrases which can join together ideas. Some of the commonest are 'and', 'but', 'or', 'in other words', 'finally', 'nevertheless', 'just then', 'as soon as'.

consonant

There are 21 consonants in the alphabet:

b, c, d, f, g, h, j, k, l, m, n, p, q, r, s, t, v, w, x, y, z.

The rest are vowels.

dash

A dash holds words apart. It is stronger than a comma, but not as strong as a full stop:

There is only one meal worth eating – spaghetti!

It is longer than a hyphen which links words together:

I love freshly-baked bread.

derivation

The derivation of a word is where the word comes from. It is often possible to find out which language the word comes from.

Portable comes from a Latin word. (*Portare* means 'to carry'.)

figurative language

This is language which uses similes and metaphors (figures of speech) to create an impression or a mood:

She **flew** down the stairs.

The opposite of figurative language is when a description is **literal** – it describes something as it actually is:

He **flew** to Spain on a jet.

homophone

These are words which sound the same but are spelled differently. They also mean very different things.

paw poor pour   road rowed rode

imperative

A verb which is in the imperative is a command:

Get me a drink and **switch** on the television.

What is really meant is 'You get me a drink', but the pronoun 'you' is not said.

letter string

This is a string of letters which always stays the same in spelling. Letter strings may not always make the same sound in words:

ough   rr   gue   qu

metaphor

A metaphor is a comparison of two things. In a metaphor, we do not say that one thing is *like* another. We say it *is* something else.

The moon is a ghostly galleon.

He is an ass.

mnemonic

A mnemonic is a useful way to remember something. It might be a rhyme:

Thirty days hath September, April, June, and November...

or it could be a handy phrase:

A Rat In The House May Eat The Ice Cream can help you to remember how to spell 'arithmetic'.

There's a RAT in Separate is a helpful way to remember a tricky spelling.

noun

A noun is a naming word. It can be the name of a person, place or thing (a common noun), e.g.:

a **girl**, the **park**, a **dragon**.

It can be a proper noun – the name of a particular person, place or thing – in which case it will have a capital letter, e.g.:

France, Jenny.

It can be a collective noun – the name of a group of things or people, e.g.:

a **swarm** of bees, an **army**, a **flock**, a **herd**.

Nouns can also be abstract – these are feelings or ideas, e.g.:

love, jealousy.

passive (form of the verb)

A verb is passive when the action of the verb is being done to the subject by someone or something else in the sentence. It often uses phrases such as 'was' and 'were':

The car **was** driven by Fred.

The car is the subject of the sentence. The verb 'to drive' applies to the car and not Fred. (See active form of the verb)

person (of a verb)

When writing, we can use verbs in singular or plural.

singular:

the first person – **I** said, **I** make

the second person – **you** said, **you** make

the third person – **he** said, **she** said, **it** makes

plural:

the first person – **we** said, **we** make

the second person – **you** said, **you** make

the third person – **they** said, **they** make

phrase

A phrase is a part of a sentence. It usually consists of two or more words. It cannot make sense by itself as it does not have a verb:

The fog crept **through the streets**.

prefix

A prefix is a group of letters that are added to the beginning of a word to change its meaning:

happy can become **un**happy

way can become **sub**way.

prefixes

preposition

This is a word which usually shows the position of one noun to another:

The cat sat **on** the mat.

The car drove **over** the bridge.

prepositions

proverb

This is a traditional phrase or expression used to teach a kind of lesson. It is not literal (true). They are commonly known and are considered to be wise:

People in glass houses shouldn't throw stones.

pun

A pun is a joke. It plays around with words that have more than one meaning. They usually have the same sound:

Where are the general's armies? They are up his sleevies!

root (of a word)

This is a word to which prefixes and suffixes can be added:

Clear can become un**clear** and **clear**ly.

root

semi-colon

A semi-colon is a punctuation mark used to separate parts of a sentence. It is stronger than a comma but not as strong as a full stop:

Shirin loves Indian food; Marco prefers Italian food.

↑
semi-colon

simile

A simile is a comparison. The writer compares one thing to another using the words 'like' or 'as':

to swim **like** a fish

as happy **as** a lark

suffix

A suffix is a group of letters added to the end of a word:

Soft can become soft**ness** and soft**ly**.

suffixes

superlative

When we say something is at its greatest, we use a superlative:

loud, louder, **loudest**

Sometimes words use a different form:

the **most beautiful**

Words such as 'good' are peculiar and have their own forms:

better, **best** (See comparative)

syllable

Longer words may be broken down into smaller parts called syllables:

Bad has one syllable; **bad/min/ton** has three syllables.

synonym

These are words with the same meaning, or very similar meanings:

hot, boiling, steaming, scorching

tense (of a verb)

The tense of a verb tells us when something is happening in the past, the present or the future:

present: now I see my mum

past: yesterday I saw my mum

future: tomorrow I will see my mum

thesaurus

A thesaurus is a book containing lists of words of similar meanings (synonyms). The words are arranged in alphabetical order.

verb

A verb is a doing or a being word:

The cat **scratched** my hand.

The cat **was** asleep.

vowel

There are five vowels in the alphabet – **a, e, i, o, u**. The letter **y** makes a vowel sound in some words. Most words contain at least one vowel. (See also consonant). Vowels can be pronounced long as in '**a**ce' and '**i**ce' or short as in '**a**nt' and '**i**n'.